GAME "ON"

GAME FACE

AN ATHLETE'S GUIDE TO
INNER MASTERY AND OUTER VICTORY

Theone Press · Princeton, New Jersey

THEONE PRESS
Princeton, New Jersey

All rights reserved
Copyright © 2012, 2021 by Jonathan Star

No part of this book may be reproduced without written permission from the author. For contact information, go to: JonathanStar.com

ISBN 9: 0-9754792-1-0
ISBN 13: 978-09754792-1-6

***

SPECIAL THANKS to everyone for their inspiration, support, and help, including: Randolph Rothey, Ed Tseng, Elemer Boreczky, Gina Amoroso, Teressa Tunney, Orrin Star, Mark Robbins, Rick Goeke, Lazlo Nyitrai, John Longo, Mr. "T," and the Hurleyville Crew (including Corey G., Andre, Cody, Eddie, Brandon, Jonathan, and Vinnie).

Note: The arrow symbol [→] indicates that additional information on the subject can be found at the website: GameOnLife.weebly.com.

To everyone I ever played with,
Everyone I ever learned from, and
The Spirit within that ever leads us to greatness.

Contents

Introduction   1

BOOK ONE:
KEY APPROACHES TO MENTAL MASTERY & THE STATE OF "ON"

1. FORM THE RIGHT RELATIONSHIP WITH YOUR THOUGHTS   9
    Belief in the Realness of Thought
    You are Not Your Thoughts
    Two Approaches to Thought

2. MASTER THE MOMENT   19
    The Present Moment
    The Breath
    Let Go and Let Golf

3. GET BEYOND THE COGNITIVE MIND   29
    Understanding Your Higher Mind and Lower Mind
    Mastering the Free-Throw in Basketball

4. ALIGN WITH LIFE   35
    Dharma / Natural Law
    Stay with the Positive
    Self-Inquiry and "On" Work
    Raising Your Life-Vibration

5. DISCOVER AND EXPRESS YOUR CREATIVE POWER   43
    The "Secret" of Creative Manifestation
    Giving Life to Our Creation
    Playing from the End

6. RESOLVE THE PAST / RESHAPE THE FUTURE   51
    Athletic Trauma
    Conscious Retrieval
    Creative Revision
    Revising Your Day

7. ADOPT A WINNING MINDSET   67
    Embrace the Positive
    Don't Play Against an Opponent
    Play with Effortlessness and Ease
    Enjoy the Game
    Adopt the Mindset of a Champion

8. MEDITATE (ACCESS THE CORE OF YOUR BEING)   77
    Meditation
    Three-fold Awareness Practice
    The Constant of Presence

BOOK TWO:
QUESTIONS & ANSWERS

I. THE STATE OF "ON"   93

II. THE MENTAL, PHYSICAL, AND SPIRITUAL GAME   108

    Appendix (Conscious Retrieval)   127
    Bibliography   129
    About the Author   130

Introduction

> I felt a strange calmness I hadn't experienced in any of the other games. It was a type of euphoria; I felt I could run all day without tiring, that I could dribble through any of their team or all of them; that I could almost pass through them physically. It was a very strange feeling and one I had never felt before. Perhaps it was merely confidence, but I have felt confident many times without that strange feeling of invincibility.
> (Pelé, *My Life and the Beautiful Game*, p.57)

Every so often an athlete rises to a level of performance where he's in the zone, flowing, or on his game. In this state he often feels as if some higher force is guiding his actions, infusing his every move with mastery and grace. There's a feeling of power and an uncanny sense that one can do no wrong. Time even seems to slow down. This wondrous and seemingly mystical state is called *the zone, the flow,* or *the state of "on."*

What draws an athlete into this state is often viewed as a mystery. It's something that happens on rare occasions and seems to come about by some auspicious, yet unknown, convergence of forces. But is this state really a random occurrence or an act of grace? Is it brought about by some "x factor" or is its cause something we can discover? And, if so, can we take deliberate steps to enter this state on a consistent basis?

Many books have been written about the zone; and the major strategies offered for getting into this state involve a kind of reverse engineering where the outer qualities of the zone are duplicated in an attempt to draw its inner dimension. And, yes, embodying these outer qualities may incline an athlete toward the zone but it can never actually deliver the state. Something more is needed. Reaching the zone involves an inner shift, an integration of body, mind, and spirit; an opening to a higher dimension of self. It is not something we can access on demand or by an act of will; however, it's a state we can incline ourselves toward, and access more and more, through informed and diligent practice.

Entering the State of "On"

The first time I entered the state of "on" came after having had a profound harmonization of body, mind, and spirit. Some internal shift had led me to a deep sense of well-being; I sensed that everything was in its perfect place, that life was good, that all kinds of possibilities existed for me. Later that day, when I went to play soccer, I noticed that this sense of well-being and "alrightness" had opened to a state of wonder and euphoria. Everything I did was in flow with Life; and in this state of flow I could do no wrong. I saw where I wanted to kick the ball and there it went. I aimed for the top-left corner of the goal, and that's where the ball landed. Sometimes I just intuited where I wanted to shoot the ball, without having a precise direction, and some force would seemingly take over and guide the shot through me. There was a direct connection between my mind and my body; a direct translation of my intention into action— and yet there was something more. At times I would take a step back and revel in the amazement of it all, in the grace and beauty that was pouring through me.

The state continued after the game and for the rest of the day; however, three days later, when I went to play again, it was gone. My mind and its usual concerns were again in the forefront of my awareness. Try as I may, I didn't have the stuff. In the game I was in three days earlier I recall a moment where I felt enveloped by golden light. This feeling had nothing to do with being in the zone, per se, but somehow that image came up for me. So, in an attempt to get back to the same state I was in before, I went to the sideline and visualized being surrounded by this golden light. After holding this image for a minute or two, and entering the expanded feeling it invoked, I got wind of the state I was in a few days before. That small amount of centering brought about some harmonization of my psyche because when I returned to the game there was a noticeable improvement in my play. I was not in the state of flowing grace as I was in before but I was again on the top of my game.

Formula for the Zone

> The zone has been a state that athletes have not been able to enter at will. The array of mind/body training techniques and perspectives practiced by athletes and taught by sport psychologists serve to increase the possibility of achieving a zone state, but they do not guarantee it. Rick Wolfe said, in response to the question, "How do you get in the zone?"—"If I knew that I'd be a millionaire many times over."
> (Cooper, *Playing in the Zone*, p. 37)

The zone cannot be separated from life; and a key understanding about moving toward the zone is this: The more deeply you enter life and embody your inherent state of aliveness, joy, and well-being the more consistently you move toward the zone. Stating this in more formulaic terms, we could say that the way to move toward the zone is a) to have a mind that is firm yet flexible, concentrated yet open to the influx of your higher self; and b) to align yourself with the positive flow of Life and the joyous calm and power of your own being.

Understanding this is easy. Doing it—getting past your mind and all its limitations—is rather difficult.

In *Game On* this basic formula for moving toward the zone is expanded into eight fundamental approaches. Each approach can be seen as a mini-formula for the zone, a mindset for inner mastery, and an entryway into the luminous state of your higher self. These eight approaches are as follows:

1) *Form the Right Relationship with your Thoughts.* When we form the right relationship with our thoughts we come to realize that *we are not our thoughts* but the conscious presence that is aware of our thoughts. When we gain this perspective we're in a better position to accept (and respond to) the thoughts we want and to "let go" of (and not respond to) those we don't want. This chapter explores ways to form a positive relationship with your mind, to minimize the effects of negative thoughts while maximizing the benefit of positive ones.

2) *Master the Moment.* Everything takes place is the present moment; and the more we can occupy the present moment the more we can exert a positive influence over our lives. This chapter outlines a few approaches by which an athlete can stay centered in the present moment, with an emphasis on conscious awareness and the breath.

3) *Get Beyond the Cognitive Mind.* Our cognitive mind enables us to learn new things and perfect our skills but at some point—if it's too much in command of our actions—it can undermine our performance. This chapter outlines ways in which an athlete can move beyond the sway of his cognitive mind and gain access to his higher, intuitive mind. The primary approach involves cultivating a cognitive mind that is open and firm, involved in the action but not in total control of it.

4) *Align with Life.* When we come into positive alignment with Life we draw all the qualities of Life—including aliveness, power, and grace—and incline ourselves toward the zone. This chapter outlines the essential understanding and approach by which an athlete can come into resonance with Life and his higher self.

5) *Discover and Express your Creative Power.* The zone is not a passive state; it is not something that happens—it's some-

thing we create whether we are aware of it or not. When we're able to "own" and direct our creative power we can reliably move toward the zone and help create that state (rather than just letting it come when it will). This chapter outlines the nature of the creative power and outlines several ways that an athlete can use this power to uplift his play and his life.

6) *Resolve the Past / Reshape the Future*. Most of our reactions to life are unconscious and based upon painful memory-blocks stored in our subconscious mind. These blocks usurp our power and thwart our sense of aliveness and joy. This chapter explores the nature of these blocks (especially as they relate to loss in athletic events) and provides strategies for dissolving their negative, emotional effects.

7) *Adopt a Winning Mindset*. This chapter explores five mindsets that are integral to the zone and mastery of the mental game. These are: a) *Embrace the positive* (as all transformation comes through the positive); b) *Don't play against an opponent* (rather focus on the highest in yourself); c) *Play with effortlessness and ease* (and not with strain and struggle); d) *Enjoy the game*; and e) *Adopt the mindset of a champion*.

8) *Meditate (Access the Core of your Being)*. Meditation is the primary means by which a person can move beyond the fluctuations of the mind and establish an immovable center at the core of his being. This chapter outlines the fundamentals of meditation as well as the practice of presence, which involves the integration of the meditative state with one's daily activities.

Mastery and the Mental Game

> Ninety percent of the game is half mental. ~Yogi Berra

Every athlete from the high school player to the professional hears the same thing: the athletic contest is 60% mental and 40% skill. This is basically what I heard from my coaches in high school but I think their formula was 80% mental and 20% skill. Everyone agrees that the mental game is vital but so few people know how to train for it and even fewer have the wherewithal to master it. So an athlete may practice for long hours and perfect his physical game but without mental mastery he is still at the mercy of his mind, his thoughts, and his uncertain reactions to all that takes place in his environment; and he never gains direct access to his true power or potential.

Mental mastery is a life path. It's not something one can attain with a few quick-fix methods. It's not something one can leave up to chance and hope that one day it will happen. To become a master of the mental game (and life itself) one must understand the key elements of the mental game, be dedicated to mastering his own mind, and do what is needed to embody these higher principles. One must become a "higher athlete." One must find value in something greater than merely winning, or attaining admiration, or appeasing some personal desire, or receiving some reward. One must have the intention to master his game, his life, and Life itself. Like a true master of the martial arts, an athlete must gain mastery over every dimension of his being—body, mind, and spirit. The rest, then, will naturally manifest in the highest most beneficial way. Victory in an athletic contest, though not the primary goal, will be the inevitable result of such inner mastery, of having achieved victory over oneself.

> I may win and I may lose, but I will never be defeated.
> ~Emmitt Smith

• • •

BOOK ONE:

KEY APPROACHES TO MENTAL MASTERY AND THE STATE OF "ONE"

Chapter One:
Form the Right Relationship with Your Thoughts

The first step toward mental mastery involves looking within; becoming aware of the thoughts that pass through your mind; understanding the concepts, beliefs, and assumptions you hold to be true, and knowing how they prompt your actions and reactions to life. This kind of inquiry is called, "inner work." When we become more conscious of the workings of our psyche it puts us in a position of choice over our thoughts and affords us greater power over our life. If we like where we are, what state we're in, we can expand that state; if we don't like where we are, we can take steps to change things. If, however, *we don't know where we are*, if we don't know what's prompting us to act, then we can't do much; we can't make any definitive changes. Our only option would be to try and change things on the outside and hope for some good results. But this approach does not get to the root of the issue and is somewhat backwards. That's because the inner is the prime determinant of the outer: How you feel about yourself and what you hold to be true largely determines the quality of your life and the conditions of your outer world, not the other way around.

Belief in the Realness of Thought

There's a saying, "Thoughts can make you and thoughts can break you"—and this is true to the extent that you *believe in the realness of your thoughts*. One thing you should understand is that thoughts in and of themselves are never the problem. It's our belief in the realness of thought, our identification with thought, our total involvement with thought, and the way we allow thought to dictate our inner state that presents us with difficulties. The oft-quoted line from Proverbs, "As a man thinketh in his heart, so he is," sheds some light on this truth. This line does not say "as a man thinketh so he is" (or "the way a man thinks determines the quality of his life") it says "as a man thinketh *in his heart*, so he is." In other words, it's only those thoughts that we believe, that we "take to heart," that determine our experience and shape our life. Thoughts that we do not embrace, that we do not hold in our heart, do not command any real power over us. Thus, the only power that thoughts have over us *is the power we give to them*. The less power we give to thought, the less we "buy into" the content of our thoughts, the less power they have over us, and the more power we have to determine our fate and the course of our life.

You are Not Your Thoughts

In the process of gaining mastery over your own mind, the first principle to truly understand is that you are not your thoughts, or emotions, or anything else that arises in your mind. (You're something much greater but we'll get to that later.) When working with your thoughts you have to recognize and experience the clear difference between who you are and the thoughts that arise in your mind. You have to break your long-standing identification with thought. You have to "step back" and create some psychological distance between you (the conscious observer) and your thoughts. And to do this you have to be more conscious of the thoughts that arise in your mind (and also your habitual reaction to those thoughts) and less unconscious when it comes to your own thinking. You can only change that which you are aware of (and never that which you are unaware of).

In this process of taking a step back (i.e., in creating some distance between you, the observing consciousness, and your thoughts) you need to put your thoughts in perspective and not assign so much importance to the content of thought while assigning more value to your inner presence that is beyond thought. You are stepping back from your involvement with thought to that conscious center at the core of your being, that place where you already reside. The more you become aware of and empower that center of self, that "place" from which you view your thoughts—through meditation, introspection, and various other practices—the easier it will be to step back from your thoughts and disidentify with the content of your mind. See thoughts as thoughts; be in a position of choice where you can accept or not accept a thought; and always remember that you are not your thoughts.

Thoughts as Suggestions not Commands

When working with your thoughts, it's often useful to see them as helpful suggestions (provided to you by your subconscious mind) rather than as directives or commands you must follow. I learned this lesson while working on my first book, *The Inner Treasure*, which was published by Bantam Books in 1992. When the manuscript was complete I sent it in to my editor and a few weeks later I received it back with funny-looking editorial marks scribbled all over it. As I began to read the edits I started to get agitated. I did not agree with a lot of them and did not want to incorporate all of the edits into my book. (Some of the edits I liked, and found useful, but not all of them.) I didn't know what to do. I was a first-time author and these edits had come from professionals at Bantam; and I was somehow under the impression that I *had to* accept every edit, as written. So I sat and thought about it for a while. Finally I adopted the position that these edits should be viewed as "suggestions" and not as commands. I was the author; I could accept the edits I liked and pass over the edits I did not like. And that's what I did. Suddenly I had power over the edits and my authorial destiny; the edits no longer had power over me.

This is the kind of relationship we want to form with our own thoughts—to see them as suggestions from our subconscious mind—ones that we can accept or reject—and not as commands we must follow. Accepting every thought that comes to us is like being a golfer who blindly accepts every club his caddy gives to him without realizing that he has a choice, that he can accept a club if he wants it and reject a club if he doesn't want it. After all, he is the golfer; he is playing the game, not his caddy. [→ See website for more information.]

Two Approaches to Thought

When working with your thoughts there are two fundamental approaches you can take. The first is to consciously change your negative thoughts to positive ones. For this you must be diligently aware of your thoughts and thought patterns and constantly "checking" yourself to see what thoughts are arising; and each time you catch yourself dwelling on the negative side of things consciously shift your thoughts toward the positive. The second approach is to abide in a dimension of self that is beyond thought; and from that place of stillness allow your thoughts to be. Rather than being pulled in the direction of every thought—even with the positive intention to change a bad thought to a good one—simply allow a thought to be as it is, without getting involved, without reacting, and without feeling the need to change it. To do this you must begin to place more importance on the one who is observing the thoughts and that center of awareness beyond thought then on the thoughts themselves (and their content.) Just be aware of the thought, as a thought, from that place of awareness beyond thought.

Bear in mind that you cannot fully enact these approaches if you're totally identified with your thoughts. You must have some access to a place within your self that is beyond thought. Trying to change your thoughts (and the pattern of your thinking) when you're still identified with them is like trying to move a carpet while you're still standing on it. Not so easy.

The Zen Approach of "Not Handling" Negative Thoughts

The Zen approach of not "handling" negative thoughts (and emotions) is to not handle them at all but to simply be aware of them. (The emphasis is on allowing thoughts, not reacting to thoughts, putting forth no effort to change thoughts. Just be with your thoughts and become more and more aware of the one who is aware of the thoughts.) This may seem counter-intuitive but we cannot get rid of the negativity of a negative thought by focusing on it, by trying to change it, by "handling" it; and the more we react to a negative thought, the more we empower it and the more we get those kinds of thoughts in the future. We can ultimately move beyond the influence of thought by anchoring ourselves in a higher dimension of self and, from there, allowing thoughts to be, just simply being aware of them. As we do this, as we live from the immovable center of our being, and no longer react habitually to every thought (especially the negative ones), our mind begins to slow down. Moreover, the thoughts that do come are more positive, more uplifting, and more aligned with our higher self.

Thought Dude and Presence Dude

To gain a better understanding of what it means to "not handle" your thoughts let's use the help of an analogy. Imagine that there are two rooms (separated by a glass wall) with *Thought Dude* in one room and *Presence Dude* in the other. Now, let's say you wake up one morning and find yourself in the room with Thought Dude. (In real life, this is what actually happens: the moment you wake up in the morning, even before you get out of bed, your thoughts start to kick in and you enter a world of thought; and that is where you remain for the rest of the day.) So you're in the room with Thought Dude and he's all over the place; he's talking, then he's singing a song you just heard on the radio, then he's reminding you of the stuff you have to do, then repeating your usual concerns, then he's talking to himself, then he's talking to someone who's not even there! This guy is non-stop. He's blathering in your ear from the moment you wake up until you go to sleep. (And quite often his blathering will keep you up at night.) You really can't get away from him for more than two-seconds at a time. (But, oddly enough, you're so used to all this noise that you barely notice it; more than that, you think it's normal.) Now in the other room is Presence Dude. This guy is chillin'. He's in the groove, he's flowing. He's always in a state of peace and calm (yet underneath he's also vibrant and alive). So, how do you get into *that* room? For now, let's say you have a special pass and you can go into that room whenever you like. So there you go, into the room with Presence Dude. Now, for the first time, you're in a state of peace and calm. You're in the zone. Thought Dude is no longer blathering in your ear and grabbing all your attention. You're feeling a sense of your inherent aliveness and joy. Now you look through the glass wall and you see (and just barely hear) Thought Dude doing his thing, making all kinds of negative comments, finding faults in other people, telling you that you're no good—and you don't like any of that. So now what? Well, you can use your special pass to go back into the room with Thought Dude to stop him from saying all those bad things (and also to try to get him to say good things) but do you really want to do that? Do you really want to leave the room with Presence Dude and go back in there with Thought Dude—even if it is to change his ways from bad to good? Why do you even care about what Thought Dude is doing or saying? What if you remained with Presence-Dude and simply allowed Thought Dude to do whatever he wanted without reacting to it, without feeling compelled to try and change things? Well, you can do just that. You have a choice. Nothing is forcing you to go back in there with Thought Dude (even though, through force of habit, you may feel compelled to do so). You can remain in the room with Presence Dude, in touch with your own presence and joy, and simply allow Thought Dude to do what he's doing, without getting involved. (And by the way, ninety-nine percent of what Thought Dude is saying is repetitive, nonsense, which has no value to you). Now, if you don't go back in there, if you don't assign too much value to Thought Dude and what he's saying, well, all that talk begins to slow down. Unbeknownst to you, the more attention you give to Thought Dude the more he blathers on. It's your constant involvement with Thought Dude (or what we might call "Monkey-Mind Dude") that empowers him. Don't get so involved with Thought Dude, or try and change his actions, and he'll begin to lose his power over you. He'll take a nap. But don't worry—he will instantly awaken the moment you need him to think some important thoughts for you.

When contemplating this analogy, bear in mind that *you are Presence Dude*. That's your true self. However, you've been stuck in the room with Thought Dude for so long that you forgot who you are—now you *think* you're Thought Dude!

"Not Handling" Negative Emotions

Should we handle our emotions or not handle them? Should we look at them like a disinterested witness, as we can do thought, or do we need another approach? This is where the idea of "mental toughness" may come in; it's the ability to not let emotions derail your game, to be tough in the face of adversity. Using this "tough" approach with minor emotions and upsets, when you're in the middle of a game, as a way to prevent them from derailing you, can be helpful but applying this same strategy to all emotions, particularly strong and persistent emotions, can be problematic.

Our first inclination or knee-jerk reaction to a painful emotion (and to the uncomfortable physiological response it elicits) is to try and get rid of it, push it under, ignore it, or drown it out. As a defense strategy we often supplant the emotion with a mental reaction to the emotion, with a running commentary on the emotion, and this effectively cuts us off from feeling the actual emotion. But these ways of "handling" emotions or toughing through them does not work in the long run. Deeper and more traumatic emotions don't respond very well to being ignored or "handled"; the more you ignore them the louder they will cry out. So, we can't just ignore emotions or look at them disinterestedly and hope they'll go away. They won't. The way to deal with such emotions is to *feel them* and not to try and suppress them, ignore them, or dismiss them. You want to feel the pure sensation of the emotion in your body. Where is it arising in your body and what does it feel like? You may discover that all strategies to avoid an emotion, and all your negative reactions to an emotion, end up being more painful than the emotion itself. So don't react, don't comment, feel.

I understand this approach when it comes to negative thoughts and emotions—but what about positive ones? What should we do, or not do, in response to them?

The highest approach to positive emotions is to accept them *as they are*, in and of themselves, as expressions of your own nature, and not conjoin or link them to some outer event or condition. Take away the eliciting event, take away the great shot that brought about your joy, and simply experience the joy as it is. If you can do this, if you can revel in that pure joy, with nothing added unto it, or nothing curtailing it, it naturally expands. That's because joy, along with every positive feeling, is in resonance with your being and boundless by its very nature.

What does it mean to say "yes" or "no" to a thought? Is there any value in literally saying "yes" or "no" to a thought?

You don't actually say "yes" or "no" with your mind's little voice—even though this approach may have some usefulness at the beginning. Primarily, you say "no" to a thought *by not reacting to it*, by not identifying with it, by not accepting it as such, by not allowing it to have any affect on you. You say "yes" to a thought when you accept it and identify with it, when you react to it, when you try and change it, and when you allow it to shape your consciousness or affect your actions.

Most of the time this is an unconscious process; we habitually accept or say "yes" to our thoughts without realizing it. Even our attempt to go in there and change a thought—well, before we do that we first have to say "yes" to that thought.

Many sports psychologists believe that a player should try and keep his emotions in check during a match; that he should not let anything affect him, neither good shots nor bad ones. This seems to be the approach taken by Roger Federer. Is this the approach that "higher athletes" should adopt?

The idea of keeping all emotions in check is what we might call a Stoic approach. This is where a player tries to eliminate the emotional component of his game and become more matter-of-fact, more technical, more immune to the ups and downs of his emotions. (Some people think of this as the Zen approach, however, the Zen approach is more about allowing an emotion to be, and centering your awareness in a place beyond emotion, than about not feeling anything.)

Being able to hold your emotions in check may be very helpful for players who get derailed by their emotions, and it is a very good first step in mastering the mental game, however, it's not likely to inspire the highest level of play or move a player toward the state of "on." With this matter-of-fact approach a player may lose the animating power of his emotions and get cut off from his own aliveness. This, of course, is preferable to being derailed by your emotions; however, the highest aim is not to try and eliminate emotion but to move beyond the sway of negative emotions while consciously expanding the influence of positive ones; and, all the while, accessing a power within you that is beyond thought and emotion altogether.

A player who wants to master his game and his life has to be careful with a non-feeling approach; any approach that cuts you off from your emotions may also cut you off from the vibrancy of life. In addition, when you forcefully decide *not to feel* or not to experience a negative emotion, that emotion does not go away; rather it just gets pushed into your subconscious mind where you do not experience it directly but where its negativity continues to influence you unawares.

As you begin to master the mental game, you slowly get in touch with a dimension of self that is more central to your being than emotion. For example, aliveness, joy, and euphoria—all of which are integral to the state of "on"—are not, in essence, emotions, they are qualities of your own nature. The state of "on" is supported by positive emotions, and thwarted by negative ones, but this state of attunement with your higher self is something beyond emotion. It is deeper, more central to the core of your being than emotion. Play from there.

● ● ●

Chapter Two:
Master the Moment

Now is the moment of power. ~Huna saying

Nothing is more powerful than right effort put forth in the present moment. ~*The Yoga Vashishta*

The Present Moment

Everything we seek is found in the present moment. All aliveness is found in the present moment; all creative power is found in the present moment; all joy and fulfillment is found in the present moment; and all victory is found there as well. The state of "on," which is the state of your higher self, is only accessible in the present moment. That is where you want to be.

Cultivating a Proper Relationship with the Past

One thing we can be sure of: the past was not different from what it was. Maybe it *could have been* different and maybe it will seem different (in the future) but the past, as it occurred, was exactly as it was. It cannot be changed. The only thing we can change is *our relationship to the past* and our reaction to the past, and that takes place in the present moment. Some people believe that the sum total of every factor in life brought about the events of the past exactly as they were supposed to be; and that the past could not have been any different from what it was else it would have been different. If a person holds this view it does not mean he has to like the past only that he has no choice but to accept it as it occurred. And this full acceptance of the past often makes it easier to let go of past events, thus enabling a person to be more in the moment and better able to work toward a positive future. Bear in mind that the past includes old childhood traumas as well as the shot you missed five seconds ago.

Regardless of your philosophical view, you never want to repeat a negative past or allow your *negative reaction to the past* to infiltrate and pollute your life in the present moment. Yet this is exactly what happens: people usually view past events with a *sustained negative reaction*. And this brings all that garbage into the present and adversely affects their future. So it's triple indemnity: negative past, negative present, negative future. How many times does a lingering lament over a missed shot, a bad call, or a blown opportunity ruin the present moment and debilitate our performance?—all too often.

Our aim, then, is to honor the moment, to station ourselves in the moment, and to let go of everything that pulls us out of the present moment, such as our thoughts (and regrets) *about* the past and our thoughts (and fears) *about* the future.

Forgiveness

One way to free ourselves from the negative influence of the past is to forgive others and our self. This is not about being religious or saintly; this is about becoming free of a burdensome past and opening to more of our aliveness in the present moment. It's about making a choice; choosing who we are and who we want to be in relationship to our own life. Do we want to fully honor the present moment and our present life or do we want to remain enslaved to the past and a past version of ourselves? Forgiveness is truly beneficial yet easier said than done, especially for a person who is ego-driven and out of touch with his true self-worth. Only a person who stands in his own greatness, in a place beyond ego and the pettiness of blame and regret, can truly forgive himself and others. Only such a person can fully come into his own power and feel the wonder of life as it is unfolding now. You must understand what version of yourself you are holding onto when you refuse to forgive—and that is the hurt, three-year old version of yourself. That is the small, boxed-in, ego-driven version of self. Is that really the version of yourself you want to be, now and in the future?

So long as you are not able to forgive, so long as you wallow in feelings of guilt and regret, or anger and resentment, you remain stuck in the past and blocked from what it means to be truly alive. So long as you are not able to forgive you remain tethered to an outmoded version of yourself and are never able to *be* yourself or "come into your own." In that contracted state the zone and the joy of life remain far away.

You must consider the loss that comes when you hold a grudge or wallow in guilt and regret—and that's the loss of the present moment; that's the loss of your repose, your aliveness, and your connection to Life. Such is a life deprived of true joy and well-being. When you hold onto your old, unforgiving self your priorities are out of joint with Life; you place more value on your ego and your attachment to the past than on your aliveness, joy, and true magnificence, now. For someone intent on mastery, or just wanting to enjoy life, this inability to forgive (and this refusal to let go of the past) is too high a price to pay, too high a sacrifice to make. To gain the present moment and enjoy the bounty of life we must let go of the past and forgive others and ourselves. There is no easy way around this one.

Enter the Spirit

When Spirit creates this universe there is no division, no holding back; it enters its own creation with the fullness of its being. Its existence and its creation are one and the same.

Likewise, to realize the fullness of our creative power and our life we must enter the spirit of what we are doing. We must be "all in." There can be no hesitation, no doubt, no division, where one part of us is *in* while another part is *out*; where one part of us wants one thing while another part believes we deserve something else; where our mind is doing this, our body that, and our spirit yet something else. This is not the state of Spirit; this is a state of fragmentation and powerlessness, a state where the potency of our creative power comes to naught.

On the playing field, and in all our activities, we want to enter the spirit of what we are doing; we want to be fully present, fully engaged, and one with the animating power of Life.

> By entering into the spirit of anything we establish a mutual vivifying action and reaction between it and ourselves; we vivify it with our own vitality, and it vivifies us with a living interest which we call its *spirit*. Therefore, the more fully we enter into the spirit of all with our actions, the more thoroughly do we become *alive*. The more completely we do this the more we shall find that we are penetrating into the great secret of Life.
> (Troward, *The Hidden Power*, p. 147)

The Breath

One of the earliest mind-stabilizing strategies, popularized by the tennis great, Poncho Gonzalez, was to focus on an object, somewhere in the distance, and bring your attention back to that object between every point. Many tennis players use similar mind-focusing routines such as inspecting several balls before a serve, adjusting the strings on their racquet, placing a few stray hairs behind their ears, etc. (In baseball, a common method used by batters is to adjust the Velcro on their gloves between pitches). There is no doubt that these rudimentary methods are helpful, and that's why even the top players in the world use them; however, a more encompassing way to help stabilize the mind is through deep, conscious breathing and through regular awareness of the breath.

An essential mind-stabilizing practice is the full and conscious awareness of the breath—and not just the physical breath, which brings air into the lungs, but also the "inner breath," the *feel* of the breath, which brings life-force into your whole being. The breath serves as an ideal stabilizing method or "constant" because, for one thing, we are always breathing—well, most of the time. So this is not something we have to create or do; we simply need to become aware of what is already taking place. The breath itself is not the constant so much as our regular awareness of it. When we bring our awareness to the breath our breathing naturally becomes more rhythmic and stable; and when our breath is rhythmic and stable it calms our mind, balances our autonomic nervous system, and empowers our body with vital life-force. And this supports the emergence of a sense of well-being while warding off negative states such as doubt, confusion, and fear.

Conscious Breathing as a Lifestyle

Most people in our culture are improperly conditioned and breathe in a shallow, unconscious way. The breath is usually confined to the upper region of the chest in what may be called "high breathing." This is more or less a half-breath that takes in the minimum amount of air one needs to stay alive; it's not a full breath that engages the stomach and diaphragm and brings in copious amounts of air that enables someone to thrive. To make matters worse, most people breathe through their mouth instead of their nose. When a person breathes this way he takes in air but not the life-energy (or *chi*) that permeates the subtle breath. Tight clothing, poor air quality, protruding bellies, and leaning over a desk all day, make things even worse. And all those people who struggle with weight-loss: if they could only breathe properly—in a way that balances out the positive and negative elements of the body—they could do away with most, if not all, of those burdensome diet regimes.

Making a fundamental change in the way we breathe, moving from half, unconscious breathing to full, conscious breathing can do much to enhance our mental game. This is not difficult, per se, but it requires a conscious and sustained effort.

> When we breathe consciously we receive and digest the finer substances the air has to give; we are nourished through the conscious assimilation of these substances. When we breathe unconsciously we receive what we need to keep alive, but when we breathe with awareness we nourish the life of the soul as well. It is impossible to overestimate the importance of conscious breathing. (Helminski, *Living Presence*, p. 97)

Physical and Life-Force Breath

The breath has two dimensions: the *physical breath*, which brings air into the lungs, and the *life-force breath*, which brings life-force or *chi* into the subtle channels of the body. When we talk about "breathing into" an energy center we are talking about breathing air into the lungs while consciously directing our awareness and life-force to a specific energy center. This combination of awareness and breath creates a form of combustible energy that empowers our entire body and specifically the energy center we are focused on. And we can choose which center to focus on in accordance with the kind of energy we want to activate. For instance, if we want a greater sense of stability or groundedness we can consciously breathe into the lower belly region, or *hara*. This also calms the mind and empowers our resolve. Most meditative traditions, such as Zen and the martial arts, emphasize this energy center. Conscious breathing in the *heart region* opens us to positive emotions; and it can also be used as an antidote for negative thoughts and emotions (especially when we bring in positive, loving energy with the in-breath and let go of negative energy with the out-breath). When we need more passion, when we need to get more fully into the game, we can breathe into the *solar plexus* region (with particular emphasis on infusing the in-breath with life-energy). Breathing into the solar plexus region may be the truest form of empowered breathing. This kind of breathing radiates life-energy throughout the body. Whenever an athlete is feeling tense, blasé, stressed-out, or nervous—or needs pumping up—deep, rhythmic breathing into the solar plexus region is a good course of action. And, as always, the more you breathe into this energy center off the court the more you build up your available store of life-energy—energy that can be used both on and off the court. Solar plexus breathing is especially beneficial for women who, through years of conditioning, have a diminished power center and a misbegotten sense of low self-esteem. [→]

Let Go and Let Golf

> Competitive golf is played mainly on a five-and-a-half inch course: the space between your ears.   ~Bobby Jones

All of the principles we have been discussing in terms of the mental game and mastering the moment keenly apply to golf since this sport involves so much "free time" between shots. What does a golfer do during this free time? What is he thinking about? What is he working on? If he has no game plan then he'll just go with whatever thoughts arise in his mind and hope for the best. If his thoughts are good he'll probably play well; if his thoughts are not so good, he'll probably play poorly. In both cases, however, he is not a master of his fate but a victim of his mind. A golfer who wants to master the mental game must employ a more informed and deliberate approach during this crucial "down time" between shots.

There are two major approaches you can use. The first

would be to build up a wave of momentum, to expand and dwell upon all that is positive (while moving away from negative thoughts and emotions); and to build one positive feeling upon the next until a wave of joy, aliveness, and well-being permeates your mind, your body, and your spirit. The second approach is to be more present and more centered in the here and now, and to be disinterested in the thoughts that arise in your mind (especially the negative ones). The intention here is to be fully stationed in the present moment. Don't think about the score, don't think about your last shot, don't think about your next shot—in fact, don't think at all. Just be present. Just take your next step. Just be in the feeling of being here and now. There's a saying in Zen that goes something like, "When walking, walk—but most of all, don't wobble." In other words, be present, be exactly where you are; don't do one thing while thinking about something else; don't think about hitting when you walk and don't think about walking (or anything else) when you hit. Just walk. Just hit.

The Fundamentals

When you've mastered the present moment and are centered in the aliveness and joy of your own being the actual shot-making takes care of itself. There's nothing more to do—just hit. Doing more or *trying* to do more will only get in your way. If, however, you're not yet there, not yet "one with the moment," you can move toward this state by employing a few fundamentals. These include: a) be present in your body (not in your thoughts about your body); b) be in the *feel* of the moment (not in your thoughts about the moment); and c) be relaxed and open to the flow of life. [→]

These fundamentals are integral to golf but can also be applied to most set-shots in sport including the serve in tennis or volleyball, the free-throw in basketball, bowling, horseshoes, etc. Let's explore these fundamentals in more detail:

1. *Be in your body.* To be in your body means to have a clear sense of your body's presence and a *felt sense* of your body. This is something different from *thinking about* your body, or thinking about how you look to others, or your body image. This is about having a direct sense of your own body and its physical and energetic presence. This is embodiment.

The more your awareness is stationed in your body and its innate sense of well-being the more your body comes into harmony with your mind, the more your life-energy flows through your actions, and the more you're able to truly feel what it means to be alive. And, as mentioned, conscious breathing enhances this sense of body-presence.

2. *Be in the moment.* Feel the joy of being present and doing what you love, which is being outdoors, in a beautiful setting, with your friends, playing golf (or whatever sport you are playing). When you do what you love, and are fully present in that action, there is no division, no mental displacement; there is no fear, no distraction, and no self-consciousness, no wishing you were someplace else. In Zen, this state is called, *shikantaza*, "the mind of someone facing death." In ancient Japan, when a samurai warrior was about to engage in battle, he was fully focused. A crowd might gather around, and he would be peripherally aware of what was going on around him, but not for a moment would his central focus waiver. If he thought about who was watching him or what he was going to do later that day, he would be cut down on the spot. An athlete is not under this kind of extreme pressure but the more fully present he is, the more he becomes a "samurai athlete," the more on-point his game will be.

3. *Relax and let go.* When you're physically and mentally present (and tapped into your own sense of aliveness and joy),

it's time to relax, let go, and allow the greatness of your higher self to work through you, through the skills you have developed over the years. In other words, it's time to *let go and let golf*. Be present, be alive, feel the here and now; and from that place of stillness, clarity, and ease, just hit your shot. In Zen, this might be called, *just hitting*. Don't think about hitting, just hit. Don't be outside the shot or thinking about the shot—or about whom you might impress with a good shot, or let down with a bad shot—just hit. You have to get out of your own way and "just hit" the ball. Just be yourself, feel your own aliveness, tap into your own euphoria, be here and now—and just hit from there.

"Just hitting" is something very simple but not all that easy. In order to just hit you have to just be. And in order to just be you have to get beyond the mind which is always telling you how to be but never actually allowing you to be.

Just be. Just hit. It's the simplest thing in the world yet at the same time the most difficult.

● ● ●

Chapter Three:
Get Beyond the Cognitive Mind

Never ask Spirit to do *for* you what it can only do *through* you.
  ~Thomas Troward

The wonder of the state of "on" is not that we transcend our human nature or lose ourselves in some ethereal state but that our higher nature comes to express its grace and perfection *through us*—through our human form and our developed abilities. However, for an athlete to reach this state of perfect "skill in action" he must get past his greatest friend and his greatest foe—his own mind. Paradoxically, our mind must be able to get past itself! It must be focused yet open, firm yet flexible; it must be engaged and operational yet transparent enough to allow the light of our higher self to shine through. In this mode our cognitive mind participates and becomes a conduit for the influx of our higher mind without taking over or disrupting our skillful action.

Understanding Your Higher Mind and Lower Mind

"Know thyself" is a dictum that underlies all mastery. And to truly know ourselves we must understand our dual nature, which is comprised of our *lower mind* (or *conscious mind* or *cognitive mind*) and our *higher mind* (which includes the *subconscious mind* and the *super-conscious mind*). Not only must we understand the nature of these dimensions of mind but the dynamic interplay that takes place between them.

The *conscious mind* (or cognitive mind) is the dimension of mind that is under our personal control or will. This is the mind we most fully identify with. In fact, most people *exclusively identify* with this dimension of mind while ignoring all the other dimensions of self. The conscious mind is the foundation of our personality, cognitive ability, and learning. It is linear in its processing and operates by way of the senses. It develops and gains capacity over time and is conditioned by experience. It can initiate new actions and is able to reason (both inductively and deductively). It is the mainstay of our personal existence and the mind most people are aware of.

The *higher mind* can be seen as our individual share of Universal Consciousness. This dimension of mind is always in oneness with the Universal Mind and shares the same qualities and attributes. When our higher mind is in active operation, working through us, and activating the world around us, it can be called the *super-conscious mind* (though many people, including myself, simply use the term *subconscious mind* to denote the higher mind and all its dimensions). The operation of this higher mind is infallible and beyond human comprehension. It is virtually unlimited in terms of its creative power, however, it is always curtailed by the limits we impose upon it through our conditioned, conscious mind. (Our belief in the limitedness of our own creative power is one way we curtail its operation.) The super-conscious mind works through intuition, beyond the capacity of the physical brain and senses; it is able to process all incoming information instantaneously, in a non-linear fashion. Another dimension of our higher mind is the *subconscious mind*. This portion of the higher mind controls all of our body's autonomic functions and simultaneously supports our 80+ trillion cells. It is responsible for storing and arranging all our memories in perfect order and bringing up the most relevant memory in response to any given situation. This mind can also be seen as the "supportive mind" because it supports our body and the everyday operation of our conscious mind. (It also supports our concepts and beliefs, and always moves to manifest or "make real" what we believe and hold to be true.) The subconscious mind also takes over the operation of our repeated actions, enabling us to carry out those actions without having to think or use our conscious mind.

Our higher mind is the mind that sustains and enables everything we do yet we are not aware of this and rarely if ever identify with it. Even in the state of "on," when this mind becomes fully operational and is acting through us, we rarely recognize its source or understand that it's the glorious expression of our own nature. [→]

Interplay Between the Lower and Higher Minds

Of great interest to an athlete is the interplay that takes place between his conscious and subconscious minds, specifically how his subconscious mind takes over a repeated action and renders it effortless or "second-nature." All development and mastery involve conscious engagement and repeated action until that action is taken over by the subconscious mind. As such, mastery is not so much about inborn talent but more about deliberate practice. Research indicates that mastery of almost anything can be reached with about 10,000 hours of practice. Said another way, it takes about 10,000 hours of engagement with our conscious mind for a series of actions to be taken over by our subconscious mind. Of course, the more passionate we are in perfecting an action, the more consciously we engage in an action—in other words, the more powerful and direct the communication between our conscious and subconscious minds—the quicker that action will be taken over by our subconscious mind and the quicker we will master it.

In order to become proficient at a sport we must learn new movements and new skills. In tennis, this would involve learning how to hold the racquet, how to hit the ball, where to position yourself during a point, etc. At first, this requires effort and concentration. However, after we practice these motions over and over again they get picked up by our subconscious mind and we don't have to think about them anymore; they become effortless. We still have to use our conscious mind when it comes to overall strategy, adjusting our game, making decisions, etc., but not when it comes to executing our shots. In fact, at a certain point, after we have mastered a shot, the use of our conscious mind is the very thing that gets in our way.

Mastering the Free-Throw in Basketball

I used to play basketball at a local court in upstate New York. Most of the kids I played with were in their teens and I was usually more than double or triple their age. One afternoon I was kneed in the thigh by an overly ambitious teen and could not play for a week or two. However, after a few days, I decided to hobble onto the court to practice some free-throws. Due to the pain in my thigh I was sensitized to the *exact amount of pressure* I was applying to my leg. It was then I noticed that there were very slight fluctuations in the exertion of my thigh muscle with each shot. This was something in normal conditions I would not be aware of. Using this pain as a way to gauge my exact exertion level, I was able to stabilize my thigh movement, having it be *exactly the same* for each shot. When this variable was controlled something happened: it stabilized all the other variables in my shot. Suddenly I could not miss.

Being able to control the exact exertion level of my thigh muscle created a constant that stabilized my whole shot. But this intense focus on my thigh (which I needed to do to insure that the exertion level was exactly the same for every shot) did something else: it "side-lined" my cognitive mind, occupying it with a task *related to* the shot but *not integral to it*. I was not focused on the hoop, or the ball, or my shot—which are the things a player usually focuses on—I was focused on my thigh. This side-focus loosened the grip of my conscious mind and allowed my super-conscious mind to step in and take the shot. So, in terms of using this as a method, it may be useful to focus the cognitive mind on something *related to the main action* but not essential to it. In this way the conscious mind would feel purposeful. If it were made to focus on something unrelated to the central action it might not feel purposeful or useful and then it might be quick to get back in and take over the action.

A simple variation of this method—which can also be used for serving in tennis or batting in baseball—would be to keep your cognitive mind focused on the muscles *below the belt*. Never focus directly on the target, the ball, or the basket but exclusively on your thighs, calves, knees, leg pressure, leg movement, etc. While your cognitive mind is occupied below (and feeling useful), your super-conscious mind will be free to execute the shot above. [→]

Scott Ford uses a method that is supposed to get someone into the zone "at will." This technique (as used in tennis) involves visualizing a wall that is parallel to the net, which moves back and forth with the contact-point of the ball. Is this method similar to the ones you are suggesting?

Yes. The method used by Ford encompasses the basic elements of the method we have been discussing. To get into the zone, or reach the state of "on," we must remove our cognitive mind from center stage and allow our super-conscious mind to step in and do what we trained it to do. To do this we must shift our awareness from a steely, singular focus to a soft, open translucence. This requires a level of trust since we have to open to something we cannot comprehend or consciously control. In terms of methods, Fred Shoemaker talks about "purposeful distraction" and suggests that a golfer focus on the back of the cup while putting. Tim Gallwey uses a method called "bounce-hit" in tennis, where a player says "bounce" when the ball lands on his side of the court and "hit" when his racquet makes contact with the ball. (He also uses a method in golf called *da-da-da-da*; this is where a player says "da" at four crucial points in his swing.) The method used by Ford is to imagine a wall that moves up and down the court with the contact-point of the ball; this imaginative engagement with something *related* to the action but not integral to it effectively side-lines the cognitive mind. In addition, the focus on an imaginary wall, instead of a single point, helps to diffuse the rigid focus of the cognitive mind and opens a player to his higher mind.

Regardless of what method you use, the fundamental approach remains the same; it involves getting beyond the grip of your conscious mind and opening to your higher mind. This is supported when you focus on something related to the action but not essential to it (such as your thigh or an imaginary wall); or when you diffuse your rigid focus by being aware of several things at the same time (such as your body, your breath, and your surroundings). And beyond any method, you always want to tap into your inherent sense of aliveness and joy, and be centered in the immovable presence of your being, as this always moves you toward the zone.

• • •

Chapter Four:
Align with Life

The state of life (or pure aliveness) is synonymous with the state of "on"; and every quality integral to life—such as euphoria, enthusiasm, joy, aliveness, and wonder—is also integral to the state of "on." When you're "on" you become a living embodiment of all of your one-with-life these qualities. Hence, the easiest way to access the state of "on" (or move toward the state) is to invoke and embody one or more of these "on" qualities. For example, let's say you're "off your game." Things are not going well. You're feeling drab or lifeless or you're thrown off by negative thoughts and doubt. What can you do? (Well, first off, you don't want to focus on trying to get rid of those negative thoughts or feelings. You don't want to go further into that toxic wasteland. So just leave all that stuff alone.) The fundamental approach is to consciously invoke and embody the positive feelings of life, to gently move the whole of your psyche in that direction. And the simplest way to do this is to recall and imaginatively *re-live* a scene or event when you were truly alive, when you were feeling expanded, euphoric, and "on" your game. Imaginatively re-enter that scene, bring it to life, feel into it (with the whole of your body, mind, and heart). Feel the joy and euphoria of the event, right now, exactly as you experienced it when it was happening before. This could be the scene of you having made the winning shot in an important game, the face of someone you love, or any image that fills you with delight. The image does not matter, the scene does not matter; the only thing that matters is that you experience and feel into that deep sense of aliveness and euphoria, which is your very nature.

Dharma / Natural Law

> Wherever there is *dharma* there is victory. ~*The Mahabharata*

"On" is not simply a state where an athlete feels alive or euphoric, it's a state where he is in resonance with the boundlessness of his own nature, where he feels the wonder of Life expressing itself through body, mind, and action. The ultimate game of a higher athlete is not just to win or feel good about his accomplishments; it's about coming into resonance with the All of Life and giving expression to its sublime qualities through his own existence. And the way he can do this is by embodying the life-qualities of his own nature, by reveling in his own power, and by living a life of *dharma*.

Dharma is a Sanskrit word often translated as "truth," "virtue," or "natural law." On a philosophical level, it can be understood as the laws of nature or the principles that govern and sustain the universe. On an individual level it can be understood as one's life-purpose; but more immediately it refers to true and righteous actions—actions that bring a person into alignment with Life (or Truth).

Dharma is derived from the root, *dhr*, which means to sustain, uphold, or nourish. Accordingly, dharma is that which sustains, upholds, and nourishes the universe (as well as one's life). When we live in accord with dharma it sustains and nourishes every dimension of our being and draws the ever-sustaining power of the universe unto us. When we live in accord with dharma, we enjoy the fullness of life: our mind is clear, our heart is pure, and our actions are filled with a graceful delight. Dharma and the path of dharma lead to victory in every dimension of life, and it is a most powerful support (on and off the court) for delivering us to the state of "on."

In order to discover the actions of dharma (or the actions that align us with Life) we must first understand the nature of Life itself. What are the primary qualities of Life, besides its aliveness? Foremost, Life is positive, beneficial, and uplifting; and it always engenders more aliveness and joy. Thus, any action that is positive, beneficial, or uplifting (and brings more aliveness and joy) is an action in resonance with Life and a dharmic action, an "on" action. The very nature of Life is love; thus, any action or thought or intention that is founded upon love is a dharmic action, an "on" action. What are some of the other qualities of Life?—freedom, joy, exuberance, beauty. Any action in resonance with these qualities is, and must be, a dharmic action. Truthfulness, compassion, gratitude, certainty, and generosity are also attributes of Life; and as we embrace or express these qualities we naturally come into resonance with the All of Life and our own higher self. At this point, it should be pretty clear that every action aligned with Life, with dharma, moves us toward the state of "on."

Stay With the Positive

Cultivating positive thoughts and approaching life with a positive attitude aligns us with Life and the ever-upward movement of the universe. Why?—because Life is purely positive. We can say it a hundred times in a hundred different ways but the fundamental truth remains the same: Life is positive. All of creation is a positive expression. The first words were, "Let there be light" not "I don't want this darkness." All transformation, all gain, all success, all happiness comes through the positive. And the more we align ourselves with the positivity of Life the more we find Life's divine qualities finding expression in us.

Greatness never comes about by focusing on faults or shortcomings or by being better than someone else. The pure joy of life never comes through actions motivated by fear, anger, guilt, regret, or shame, or through an intention not is resonance with Life. All in all, we always want our thoughts and actions to be aligned with Life and the positivity of Life. And what is the surest way to do this?—be truly alive!

> It may seem a truism, but the great secret of Life is its Livingness, and it is just more of this quality of Livingness that we want to get hold of; it is that good thing of which we can never have too much. (Troward, *The Hidden Power*, p. 147)

Self-Inquiry and "On" Work

When I watch a top athlete warm up before a game (or before playing an important point) I often wonder, what is he thinking about? What is he working on? Is he thinking about the upcoming game or the shot he is about to take or what his opponent is doing? Or is he simply going with whatever subconscious thoughts happen to arise in his mind? During this warm-up time before a game (or before an important point) an athlete intent on mental mastery does not simply "go with" whatever thoughts arise in his mind. He does not allow subconscious thoughts to determine his inner state. Rather, he consciously brings himself into alignment with the highest in himself. He consciously connects with his own aliveness and generates nothing but pure and enlivening positivity.

When I go to the basketball court and practice my shots (say, before a game) the first thing I do is "on" work, or zone work, which means I take steps to align my body and mind with my higher self and the positive flow of life. I attune and sensitize myself to my inherent sense of aliveness, joy, and wellbeing. And part of this is about getting a feel for my body, my shooting muscles, and my present state of mind; and also becoming aware of any mental distractions that want to pull me out of my center. When I get into the zone—which is a self-perpetuating state—I effortlessly hit five or six shots in a row. If I don't get distracted, I hit a few more. If I think about how I am in the zone or how I'm hitting one shot after another—or wondering about who may be watching me, and how impressed they might be—I am in my mind and out of the zone. In this state I often miss the next shot. But I don't react to that miss or let it go to waste: I look at the exact thought that threw me off and seek to know how that thought disrupted my flow or cut me off from my higher self. Then I let it go and move back into the expanded state of the zone (now careful not to let the same kind of thought derail me) and shoot some more.

Doing this kind of "on" work before a game is a lot like tuning your car before a race (or tuning your guitar before a concert). Imagine what it would be like to try and tune your car *during* the race? Yet this is what most athletes do—they try to harmonize their body-mind connection and emotional state during the game (allowing the ups and downs of the game to determine their state). What we want is to get in tune with the state of "on" before the game; and then hold to that positive state during the game. Moreover, we want to keep ourselves in tune with the plenitude of Life (and the state of "on") all the time—before, during, and after the game.

Raising Your Life-Vibration

If we move beyond specific methods and techniques we find that the overarching aim of the mental game (and the game of life) *is to increase our sense of aliveness, joy, and well-being*, i.e., raise our "life-vibration level." And we can do this by attuning to our own nature and Life itself; by cultivating our highest qualities; by cultivating that which is joyful and enlivening; and by creating a positive and supportive life for ourselves—one that includes healthy living, positive and stress-free relationships, and a clear connection to a higher purpose. Conversely, we can lower our life-vibration level (and alienate ourselves from the joyfulness of our own nature) by dwelling on negative states such as fear, confusion, anger, past regrets, depression, and low self-esteem. The constant need to validate ourselves by impressing others, gaining approval, or being better than someone else also lowers our life-vibration.

The Aliveness Scale

How alive are you? How deeply are you attuned to Life? How inclined are you toward the state of "on" and your own higher self? *The Aliveness Scale* can give you some indication.

LIFE / Aliveness (The State of "On")

Love, Aliveness, Wonder, Euphoria, Bliss
Enthusiasm, Joy, Amazement, Beauty, Awe
Abundance, Fulfillment, Satisfaction, Pleasure
Expansion, Freedom, Creativity, Well-Being
Contentment, Ease, Peace, Clarity, Gratitude
Sense of Purpose, Fun and Pleasant Activities

Toward Life

Boredom, Discord, Distress, Feeling out-of-sorts
Sense of Lack, Up-Tightness, Self-Consciousness
Depression, Despair, Dis-ease, Stress, Confusion, Doubt
Frustration, Irritation, Restlessness, Unhappiness, Struggle
Misery, Grief, Anger, Hatred, Dread, Resentment
Fear, Guilt, Shame
Deadness, Apathy

DEATH / Deadness

You can use *The Aliveness Scale* to determine where you are in relation to Life. If your dominant mode or emotion hovers above the neutral line, you're inclined toward the state of "on" (and more and more Life); if it falls below the line, you're inclined toward a state of "off" (and less and less Life).

As a general practice, then, we want to "hang out" with and move toward those qualities (and emotions) that are above the line. And whenever we find ourselves in a state below the line we want to gently shift ourselves upward to a mode above the line. This is not always easy but neither is it difficult. The one mistake people often make is that they forget to be gentle with themselves; they forcefully try to get rid of a negative thought or emotion (or negatively react to being in a negative state). This brings about a mode of struggle, dissatisfaction, and self-judgment that often keeps a person locked below the neutral line. So, we want to avoid that approach. What we want is to let go of negative states *without negatively reacting to them*, or getting involved with them, or getting down on ourselves. Without a stir, just let go of where you are (and the negative state you're in) and move toward where you want to be.

The Aliveness Scale is similar to charts used in other systems, such as the emotional scale of EFT (by Gary Craig), the guidance scale of Abraham-Hicks, and the levels of human consciousness by David Hawkins.

Could you talk a little more about the practice of euphoria? Once we're able to get in touch with that euphoria (or joy or aliveness) how do we sustain it? How do we expand it?

If you use a scene or an image to help you elicit that euphoria, you can hold onto the image (if you find that to be helpful) but it is often more powerful to let go of the image and just "feel into" the pure feeling. No object, no image, just euphoria. That euphoria is your own nature; you don't need an object, image, person, or event to bring it about. If you just feel it, and hold it as your own self, and don't tether it to anything (such as some image or past event), it will naturally expand and permeate your body and mind

An important part of this process, especially when it comes to sustaining this feeling of euphoria, is to "feel into it." Feel where it is in your body; feel the effects it has on your body. Pure euphoria will envelop your whole body but it usually has an epicenter. Where is that? (It's usually in the heart or solar-plexus.) What does it feel like? (Don't use words to describe it, just feel it.) Does it have a color or a texture? Get very familiar with the "feel" of that euphoria. See how it spreads, how it fills your body (and mind) with a kind of warm glow.

Like anything else, there's no magical formula here. It requires practice. But it's fairly simple: just keep coming back to the joy and wonder that you are. As you do this, that positive joy (along with euphoria, aliveness, and wonder) will naturally expand and permeate your body, and more and more become your natural state. You will always be in the flow of life—enjoying life, reveling in life, being truly alive.

● ● ●

Chapter Five:
Discover and Express Your Creative Power

> All people possess the power to create reality but this power sleeps as though dead when not consciously exercised. Human beings live in the very heart of creation—which is the Human Imagination—yet are no wiser for what takes place therein. . . . Therefore, the individual who can summon, at will, whatever imaginal activity he pleases and to whom the visions of his imagination are as real as the forms of nature is master of his fate.
> (Neville, *The Neville Reader*, p. 3)

Most people are programmed to react to the conditions of life rather than to take considered action to create their own reality. This we might say this is an uncreative way to live. In this mode a person denies his creative power and embodies a pattern of weakness and passivity. This is not what we want. We want to create a pattern of power. We want to be in a position of creative choice and exercise that choice in a way that is beneficial and uplifting. We want to be the arbiter of our own fate not the sad victim of circumstance.

The "Secret" of Creative Manifestation

We, as human beings, possess *the power of choice* and *the power to create our reality* yet in order to enjoy the benefits of this divine power (and not unwittingly use it to our detriment) we must understand its nature and be able to intelligently direct it An important thing to understand is that our creative power is one with the Supreme Power; and that what we create, on every level, is always an act of co-creation. In this act of co-creation our role is to *consciously appropriate and "feel into" the reality we want,* and Spirit's role is to manifest that reality (as conceived and believed in by us). Four things that make way for our full participation in this process are:

1. Having a deep longing to obtain something or to make a positive change in ourselves. The purer our desire, the more our desire is in alignment with the good and positivity of Life, the more power it commands.

2. Being still, open, and receptive; having a quiet attentiveness of mind and body. We must support our creative intention with a deep receptivity and trust in Spirit.

3. Being able to imagine what we want and embracing that creation with the fullness of our being. It is *our* belief in the realness of what we have imagined, and our felt sense of that, that gives Spirit the "go ahead" to transform our imaginal creation into a living, physical reality.

4. Being open and sensitive to the operation of Spirit; and always being willing to assist Spirit in its manifestation of our desire. A major cause of failure in the creative process is when we don't rise to the occasion or act in consort with Spirit, when we expect Spirit to do *for* us what it can only do *through* us.

Giving Life to Our Creation

According to Neville Goddard, a powerful way to "give life" to our imaginative reality is to *think and live from the end.* In other words, to live as if it the reality we imagine was already a living reality and to shape our thoughts and actions upon that real—yet not yet physically manifested—reality. *We have to feel the impact* of that imagined reality (in the same way we would feel the impact of a physical reality) because our belief in the realness of our imagined creation (and our response to that realness) is what tells our higher mind to bring that into physical manifestation. Again, this is more than hope or wishful thinking, this is *the creative appropriation* of the present moment. We don't want to hold the position that our imagined reality is something that might happen in the future (or something we hope will happen in the future, like an ardent prayer) we want to go "all in" with the feeling and conviction that what we have imaged is, in fact, a living, breathing reality. If we *hope* something will happen in the future we tell our higher mind that it's not something we possess right now and, accordingly, our higher mind does not produce it for us, right now. When we feel, and react to, and believe the realness of our imagined reality our higher mind sets about to manifest it for us, now.

The extent to which our imaginal creation feels natural to us, the extent to which we "own" and feel "at home" with what we imagine for ourselves—and the extent to which it aligns with the concept we have of ourselves—to that extent does it manifest in our outer world. If you want to be a champion then you have to feel like champion, you have to be a champion, now. Winning has to feel natural to you; it's something you should always have and expect. That's how a champion thinks. You have to walk in like you own the place. And if you don't yet feel like a champion you have to appropriate that state again and again; you have to keep walking and talking and playing like a champion until being a champion feels natural to you. The secret to gaining this feeling of naturalness is repetition, positive endowment, and love; it comes by fully re-living the state you want, with the feeling of love, over and over again. If you want to be a champion you have to love the feeling of being a champion. This feeling has to become integral to your identity. When you feel like a champion you play like a champion; and the more you play like a champion the more you feel like one.

Try and try as you may, you don't always get what you want but *you always get what you are and what you believe yourself to be*. You get what feels natural to you. In other words, you always get yourself!—the self that you create. So create the self of being a champion and that's what you will get.

The Creative Power of Awareness

Most people don't realize the creative power of their own awareness; that what they choose to focus on and what they give their attention to is the very thing they enliven and create for themselves. Every human being is heir to a wondrous creative power that is activated though his own consciousness. As such, we have to be careful about the thoughts we entertain and hold in our heart. We have to be vigilant about the deep-seated beliefs and assumptions we adhere to because these are the very things that direct our awareness and create the conditions of our life. To gain mastery over our life we can't let subconscious thoughts monopolize our awareness or determine our inner state. We have to be more conscious, more creative. We have to constellate our awareness around the highest in ourselves and consciously move toward what we want (and dwell in the aliveness that we are) rather than simply moving away from what we don't want. [→]

Playing from the End

> In the art of war, a victorious army first wins and then seeks battle: a defeated army first battles and then seeks victory.
> ~Sun-tzu, *The Art of War*

An athlete can enter the heart of the creative process—and align himself with the inevitability of victory—by playing a point or taking a shot from the end and then from the beginning. To do this he must create the ideal end in his imagination and fully endow the imagined scene with the exalted feeling of having already won the point (or made the shot) before he actually plays it. And, then, this expansive and certain feeling of victory informs his play and acts as a self-fulfilling prophesy. When this art is truly mastered the vector of the point shifts from a doubtful "will I win?" or a confident "I think I will win" (or a wishful "I hope I will win") to a clear and decisive "I have won!" And that is followed by, "Now let's see by what wondrous means that victory will be accomplished."

In accordance with the law of attraction, the more powerfully we can *enter into the feeling* of having already won the point (or made the intended shot) before it is actually played the more powerfully we attract that eventuality, the more fully our super-conscious mind gets the "go ahead" to orchestrate the actions of our mind and body in order to manifest our imagined result.

It's important to remember that the conscious use of your creative power can help move you toward the state of "on" but it cannot replace it or override it. When you're "on" you're at the center-point of creation, in the now, in the effortless flow of Life. In this state, you need not consciously create anything or imagine any future result. The very act of *trying* to create something or *trying* to get somewhere—when you're already there—or here!—only separates you from the all-accomplishing flow of Life. When you're "on," just go with it, be in the wonder of it—and forget everything you ever heard about the zone, the flow, or the state of "on."

When using our imagination to "create" a shot should we imagine the entire shot in detail or just the end result?

Some visualization methods involve imagining the entire shot, exactly as you want it to be. Now this has some value, especially in terms of developing your imaginative powers, and also it can help you install a positive subconscious template, but in the creative process we have been talking about something else. Here we are talking about creating a "beacon" through the imaginal construction of a final scene (along with our complete entry into the feel and realness of that scene), not a visualization of the entire shot. We want to imagine a final scene that could only take place had we made the shot as intended; and also impart that scene with reality by responding to it in the same way we would have had the shot taken place in real life. (It is our feeling, our response to our imagined scene that makes it real to our subconscious mind, and nothing else.) This enlivened, imaginal creation extends a subtle invitation to our higher mind rather than giving it a precise directive. When we imagine something with great exactitude we don't leave any room for our higher mind to enter; we are limited to our own mental creation and cut off greater possibilities. It's like dancing with someone and telling them exactly how they should move and where they should take every step. You may end up doing the dance correctly, but where's the flow in that? Where's the aliveness and joy in that?

As a general principle, our higher mind doesn't do well with directives or commands yet *always* responds to our open invitation. We don't want to, nor can we, direct the operation of our super-conscious mind by telling it *how* to bring something about but only by showing it *what* we want it to bring about—and we do this by imagining a scene that indicates the completion of our goal, infusing the scene with a sense of realness, and responding to our imagined scene just as we would the same event having taken place in real life. After that, we step back and allow the infallible operation of our super-conscious mind to do the rest. People often fail in this process not because they are unable to create and enliven their imagined scene but because they can't get out of the way after that. They continue to think, they get impatient, they begin to doubt—and that doubt creates a counter-creation that neutralizes the efficacy of their initial creation. So they end up with nothing.

So our role in this process is to imagine, and believe in, and feel the realness of a scene, one that indicates the completion of our desired result? Can you offer a few examples?

In golf, for instance, we might imagine the ball landing in a particular area on the green. A football kicker might imagine a scene where the ball sails through the uprights (accompanied by a cheering crowd and a feeling of relief and exultation). More than having just a visual image, you could infuse your end-scene with a sound, such as the sound of the ball dropping into the cup (in golf) or the "swish" sound the ball makes when it goes into the basket. We might call this "a sound approach." Not every basket makes a swish sound but *every* time the ball makes a swish sound it indicates that a basket was made. In baseball, you could imagine the sound of the ball hitting the bat (and also the feel of it) when hitting a home run. Are you aware of the exact sound and feel of hitting a "home run"? If not, see if you can become attuned to it. See if you can forge a clear mental template of that exact sense and then use it to infuse your imaginal creation with all the tones of reality. [→]

In every case, to have manifestive power, our imagined scene must be experienced as real and must be responded to as if it were a living reality, happening right now. How would you feel if you made a decisive shot exactly as intended? Pretty great I suppose. That same feeling of elation, or euphoria, or whatever it is must be integral to your imagined scene in order to make it real for your subconscious mind. Without your full embodiment and "realization" of the imagined scene it remains moot and void of creative power. [→]

Earlier you spoke about eliciting positive emotions through the use of our imagination. If I could create this euphoria of having won an event in my mind, why bother to play at all?

Why not do both: create the euphoria in your imagination and see how that euphoria is *redoubled* when you play (and win) the event in real life? There is an extra layer of wonder and thrill that comes about when you imagine something and then watch the way it unfolds in front of you and through you—it's just as you imagined yet it's more than you could ever have imagined. That something more comes about because you have become integral to the creative process; you have entered the flow of life and joined in partnership with your super-conscious mind. All these methods and imaginings are only meant to deliver you to the state of creative fullness and life—not replace it. You want to move beyond imagining into pure play, pure joy, pure life, pure flow, and pure "on."

When a player wins Wimbledon and is standing on center court with his arms raised, where does his joy come from? Did the cheering crowd inject him with it? Was he given a joy pill? There he stands, emotionally and physically drained, yet feeling elated. So, where does that joy come from? It, of course, was with him all along but only after winning, and accomplishing his goal, did his mind (which acts like a strict gate-keeping) allow him to feel his own joy. We want to take the master-key away from the mind. We want to allow that joyous, enthusiastic, aliveness energy to infuse our game and our lives all the time. In the end, winning our own self, our own aliveness, and our own joy, is the true victory—and winning Wimbledon is not bad either.

• • •

Chapter Six:
Resolve the Past / Reshape the Future

A major part of the mental game involves becoming aware of our subconscious blocks, beliefs, fears, desires, and values, and either dissolving them or bringing them into alignment with our highest aspirations. What you will discover as you look within is that many of your thoughts and emotions are shaped by deep-seated fears, psychological complexes, childish concepts, and traumatic memories that you are not aware of. All of these limit your freedom, block your exuberance, put you off your game, and displace you from the greater flow of life. A primary aim, then, would be to free yourself from these subconscious complexes and regain your natural state of freedom and joy.

We can ignore or not react to negative thoughts as they arise but a more far-reaching approach is to become aware of and uproot the subconscious complex that gives rise to these thoughts in the first place. We can use various methods to not let fear affect us but it's a different story to not have any fear to begin with. The state of fearlessness is a state of great power and one that's inherent to the nature of our deepest self. This is the state we want to embody. To reach this state we must dissolve these deep-seated trauma-blocks and psychological complexes and the fear that so tenaciously holds them in place.

Trauma-blocks

What exactly is a trauma-block? It's a painful memory stored in our subconscious mind that carries a negative emotive charge and has the power to elicit a negative physiological reaction. These blocks can result from real traumas and deep emotional losses but also from any kind of painful event such as "growing pains," minor losses, set-backs, etc. In all cases, the greater the trauma the more power it exerts over our psyche.

Briefly stated, trauma-blocks affect us in the following ways:
a) They lower the life-vibration level of our entire psyche; they incline our thoughts and emotions toward fear, doubt, and negativity; they engender lack of confidence, low self-esteem, depression, fear, and other negative states;
b) They use up a great deal of life-energy, depriving us of the very aliveness and joy that is at the core of our being;
c) They place our subconscious mind in discord with our higher self and our higher aspirations;
d) They keep us bound to the past and out of joint with the vibrancy of the present moment.

Memory Coding

Let's explore the nature of these trauma-blocks and how they are formed. When we experience a traumatic event, either physically or psychologically, sensations and emotions related to that event get coded into our memory banks. This is part of our evolutionary self-defense mechanism and necessary for our survival. These charged, fear-based memories serve to forewarn us about similar situations that we may come upon in the future. For example, if you get bit by a dog as a child you may grow up having a fear of all dogs because the sight of a dog got coded in with the pain of that trauma. After a while, if you come to know more dogs, and none of them bite you, then that fear may get coded out of the category of "all dogs" and only apply to the specific breed of dog that bit you. If you get to know dogs of that breed and none of them bite you then your subconscious mind may eventually re-code that breed of dog and you may no longer fear dogs of that particular breed. You may only fear the particular dog that bit you—but he's probably dead and gone by now.

Although our subconscious mind picks up every sensation, only sensations that are specific to a given trauma get coded in with our memory. Using an example from sports (which usually involves an emotional trauma not a physical one) let's say a wrestler gets pinned in the finals of a major tournament that he was favored to win. (This actually happened to a friend of mine and he has never gotten over it.) The mat, the uniform, the noise from the audience, and the buzzer were all part of that devastating loss but they won't get coded into his memory because they were not *particular* to that loss. These same sensations occurred in other events and oftentimes had positive associations. However, if the opponent's uniform was of a particular color, that color might get coded in with the trauma. Whenever the wrestler sees that color thereafter it will elicit a negative physiological response. If there was a particular smell to the mat (or his opponent!) that smell might get coded in; and whenever the wrestler smells that smell it will remind him of the loss and elicit a negative response. The name of the person who beat him might get coded in and every time the wrestler hears that name (or one similar to it) he might tighten up and get a nervous feeling. Maybe the opponent was from a particular town; each time the wrestler hears the name of that town he might have a negative reaction.

With every major loss, dozens of traumatic associations get coded into an athlete's subconscious mind and all conspire to darken his thoughts, lower his sense of aliveness, infuse his psyche with fear, and degrade his overall relationship with life. As part of our mental training we want to address these traumas and take steps to dissolve the negative and fearful influence they have over our game and our life.

Athletic Trauma

One thing that is rarely addressed in sport, especially in regards to young people, is the negative affect that a traumatic loss can have on one's self-esteem, ambition, confidence level, and attitude toward life. These traumas are often far-reaching for high school and junior high school players who are emotionally fragile and still uncertain about their identity, and whose overall sense of self is very dependent upon how they are regarded by others (and how well they perform in sports). As such, a major loss in an athletic contest can thwart and enfeeble a young person's identity and sense of self-worth. Professional athletes may be better equipped to handle such a loss—in terms of their sense of self-worth—but it is still problematic in terms of their confidence level and future performance. No athlete, on any level, is immune to the ill-effects that result from a major athletic loss.

Back in grade school I wrested in a township tournament that was held every year at the end of wrestling season. I always won in my weight-class and there was no one who could compete with me. In the last year I could wrestle in the tournament someone moved into my township who could not beat me but who was, at least, in the same league as me. In a pre-tournament bout I managed to pin him but in the actual tournament we wrestled to a draw, and then to another draw. Finally there was a "judge's decision," which I lost—and with that loss my whole sense of self imploded. The rug got pulled out from under me. I was like a zombie for days or weeks after that loss. I was the guy who won the wrestling tournament every year—now who was I?

Perhaps that loss inspired me because soon after that I decided to win the New Jersey State Championship. I began to train. My coach often accused me of over-training. I had a sign on the wall of my workout room that read, *PAIN = STATE*. In my senior year I made it to the state tournament. There were two top wrestlers in the state—me and someone from a neighboring district. We were pretty even but I was favored to win; and everyone thought we were going to meet in the finals. In the early rounds of the tournament I pinned all my opponents; then came the semi-finals. I wanted to finish the match quickly, with a pin, so I would be well-rested for the finals which were going to take place later that day. Thinking more about the upcoming match than the one I was in, I made a costly error and ended up losing. Again, my whole world and my sense of self fell apart. Now who was I? The guy who could've won the state championship but didn't? (I suppose third in the state was pretty good, as no one in my high school ever reached that level, but it didn't mean much to me). I'm not clear of the extent of the damage that that trauma caused in terms of my life, my self-esteem, and my enthusiasm for life, but I'm sure it affected me for years. And my loss in the state championships had a deep effect on my fellow co-captain as well (who was the very person who beat me in that local tournament years before). He was there to support me for the whole tournament yet did not show up for the one match I lost. To this day he tells me about his regret for having let me down, feeling that if he were there to support me I would have won.

Most athletic traumas are never resolved or even addressed. Perhaps they are supposed to heal over time but they rarely do. It's just a burden that many young people carry—a burden that weighs them down and saps their zest for life. We all know that athletic programs can help children and teens build fortitude and character but the trauma resulting from a major loss, if left unresolved, can undermine most it not all of the positive gains that come from these programs. Coaches and parents should find a way to appease the negative effects that result from these losses. Talking about it, and allowing an athlete to express his or her feelings can be helpful but it's rarely, if ever, enough. Something more is needed. One process that can help dissolve some of these trauma-blocks that result from athletic loss is *Conscious Retrieval*.

Conscious Retrieval

Conscious Retrieval is a process whose origins can be traced back to Freud even though it has nothing to do with Freudian psychoanalysis. This process is rather simple but not necessarily easy. It involves imaginatively *reliving* a traumatic event over and over again—re-experiencing it fully, as if it were happening right now—until the underlying pain and emotive charge of the trauma get dissolved. In this process a person does not simply recall the trauma, or review it from an outside position, *he has to relive it*. It's precisely the pain that we do not face, that we fearfully avoid, that continues to live on and control us. Yet the very act of becoming aware of subconscious blocks transforms them. They are no longer subconscious; and through the alchemical power of our awareness these blocks, and the power they exert over us, can be dissolved.

The thing that holds these painful memories in place and keeps them entombed in our subconscious mind is fear. Our normal response to a painful event is to block it, avoid it, cloud it over, or push it away—hoping that over time the pain will disappear or recede but it never actually does. (This was the defense strategy we employed as children; and that may have worked well for us when we were five years old but it's not something that works for us now.) The pain recedes *from our conscious awareness* yet remains buried in our subconscious mind where we cannot get to it and where it continues to affect us unawares. Time covers it but does not heal it. Instead of trying to suppress or block the pain (which is our conditioned, child-based reaction) we have to go in the opposite direction. We have to face it; we have to bring it into total awareness. Only then can we finally become free of it.

When we fully experience a past trauma, *in the present moment*, it changes our experience of it *and the way it gets coded by our subconscious mind*. The fear and emotional pain get stripped away; the entire foundation that held the emotional pain in place gets dissolved. And what remains is a neutral memory of the event. Its power to bring about a fear-based, physiological response is gone. All the life-energy we heretofore used to keep the pain suppressed comes back to us and we suddenly feel hopeful, alive, and giddy. It feels as if a cloud has been lifted and we are finally ourselves again. It's at this moment we realize just how profoundly these trauma-blocks sap our life-energy and block us from the flow of our own life.

One thing to bear in mind is that our higher mind picks up everything within the field of our awareness, including a vast array of perceptions that our conscious mind does not pick up. When we recall a painful event we usually recall only those elements we were consciously aware of at the time. Yet, a lot more gets picked up and a lot more gets coded in with the trauma. So, when we go back and imaginatively relive and re-experience a traumatic event we have to become acutely aware of all the sensations and be more "in" the trauma than we were when it was actually happening; we have to become aware of all those things that were initially missed or blocked by our conscious mind (yet got registered by our subconscious mind) so that we can finally release them. (For guidelines on participating in a session of *Conscious Retrieval*, see *Appendix*.)

Creative Revision

In *Conscious Retrieval* we employ the creative power of our imagination (along with the transforming power of our own awareness) to relive a past event again and again until it is stripped of its emotional charge. Now, if we are able to use our creative imagination to re-enter a past trauma, and have our subconscious mind recode it into memory, why not use this same power to *create* a whole new reality for ourselves? Well, we can do just that! One method we can use to "go back and change the past" is *Creative Revision*. With this method the past event is not relived as it occurred; it is re-imagined and relived *as we wish it had been*. We do not accept the "reality" of the past event nor its pain (which, as of now, is just a memory). Instead, we create a new reality for ourselves. And when this newly-created reality is fully embraced and believed in *by us* our subconscious mind responds to it as being real and it gets coded into our memory banks just like an actual event. This new event, once accepted by our subconscious mind as real, is capable of *wholly replacing the old event and all its painful effects*. It's as if the original event never happened to us. We still have a memory of the event (and even recall that it was painful) but it no longer has power, its emotive charge is gone. It's like some distant event we saw on TV several years ago.

To gain a deeper understanding of how this works let's take a closer look at the nature of our subconscious mind. Earlier we explained that our subconscious mind is not able to make a decision about what is real or what is imaginary; it cannot distinguish between the experience of a physical reality and the experience of an imagined reality *that we fully believe in as being real*. (I keep repeating this point not because I want to hear myself talk but because it's essential.) Our subconscious mind relies upon *our* conscious response to an event in order to determine whether it is real or not, whether it applies to "me" or not. If we respond to an imagined scenario as real, as happening to us—in the same way we would respond to the same event in real-life—then our subconscious mind takes that imaginal creation to be real. (Likewise, if we respond to our imaginal creation as unreal, as an imaginary event, our subconscious mind responds to it in the same way as well.) So, by imaginatively recreating the original event *as we wish it to be*, and by entering into the realness of that recreated event—and emotionally responding to that imagined event in the same way we would a real-life event—and by doing this over and over again—we eventually make it real to our subconscious mind. And once this happens our subconscious mind reshapes our entire memory bank accordingly. The old event and all its painful associations get replaced (on an emotional and energetic level) by the newly-accepted event. All the life-energy that was once used to repress that painful memory suddenly returns; all the subconscious discord created by that memory gets replaced with a sense of well-being and harmony.

This approach is more advanced than Conscious Retrieval and will not be as effective when dealing with deep-seated trauma unless you have a powerful imagination, a true conviction about your creative power, and the ability to fully inhabit your imagined reality. [→]

Revising Your Shot

The power of your creative imagination can do more for you than remove trauma-blocks; it can also be used to reshape your game in a positive way. One way to employ this power would be to re-enter a game or match you played and *imaginatively recreate every shot you missed* into a shot you made. In tennis, for example, recall every key shot you missed and re-imagine instead having hit a perfect shot (and, as part of this process, feel the thrill of having made the shot just as you intended). And do this over and over again until you create a new subconscious template, until your newly-imagined shots supplant your missed shots, until all your "missed shot" templates are replaced by "made shot" templates.

After transforming all your missed shots into made shots you could then take this one step further; you could fortify your gains by imaginatively reliving every great shot you made. As you do this over and over again you will empower your subconscious templates and positively incline all your future shots toward being winners, baskets, hits, or kills.

You can use this method with baseball, basketball, volleyball and most other sports. In volleyball, for example, you would relive every contact with the ball, every set, every dig, every kill, every missed hit, over and over again, until you become very familiar with every moment of engaged play. If you missed a kill (that you could have made—or even one that you could not have made!) you would creatively imagine having made the kill exactly as intended until the thrill of it permeates your whole being. Every time you made a less-than-perfect set, you would imagine having made the perfect set, over and over again, until you cannot imagine having not made a perfect set.

In baseball you would relive every at bat, every pitch, every strike, and every hit—over and over again—until you become very familiar with each moment of engaged play. Every at bat that you did not get a hit you would creatively imagine having made a "believable" hit—a single, double, triple, or home run—until the thrill of having made that hit permeates your whole being. At the end of this process you will be reveling in the joy and confidence of having batted a thousand in your last game. And next time you're at bat your whole being will move you toward that same result.

You may think—"But this is not real. This is not what really happened. Why should I forget reality and supplant it with something imaginary?" Is your memory of an event any more real than your imagined recreation of the event? If you understand your own creative power and that the whole universe is created through the Supreme Imagination, you might see it in another way. All said, the empowered use of your imagination is how you create your reality instead of being a victim of circumstance. You have the power to create what you want if you know how to use that power. Your choice.

Revising Your Day

The creative power of your imagination can do more than just revise your game; it can be used to revise your entire life. And since your game and your life are integrally related, any improvement you make in your life will also show through as an improvement in your game.

About 2500 years ago, Pythagoras recommended to his students that they imaginatively review and complete their entire day before going to sleep. This method serves to develop our imaginative power and bring our day to a psychological completion. With this method we would imaginatively relive all the events of our day, bringing everything back into our consciousness and completing our day. [→] But we can take this practice one step further. Rather than using our imaginative power to complete our day, we can use it to re-create the events of our day—not as they occurred but *as we would have wished them to be*. Before going to sleep we would recall our day in great detail, learning and clarifying the lessons of the day, and being especially aware of any mistakes we made and how we might do things differently next time. Then we would go back and imaginatively re-live the day, *exactly as we wished it had been*, over and over again, until we create a new reality for our subconscious mind, a template for having lived the most perfect day. This would positively affect our dreams as well as our life the following day. After a while we may have less and less to revise as each day would become more and more perfect. Neville Goddard describes this method as follows:

> Now this is how we do it: at the end of my day, I review the day; I don't judge it, I simply review it. I look over the entire day, all the episodes, all the events, all the conversations, all the meetings, and then, as I see it clearly in my mind's eye, I rewrite it. I rewrite it and make it conform to the ideal day I wish I had experienced. I take scene after scene and rewrite it, revise it, and having revised my day, then in my imagination I relive that day, the revised day, and I do it over and over in my imagination until this seeming imagined state begins to take on for me the tones of reality. It seems that it's real, that I actually did experience it; and I have found from experience that these revised days, if really lived, will change my tomorrows. (Neville, Lecture, 1954)

Match Review & Revision

Athletes often review tapes of their game to see how they played and to learn how they might improve. Is this helpful? Is there something more we can do in terms of review?

Reviewing a game or match can be very helpful. But more than reviewing our game outwardly, to work on strategy and improve our performance, we want to review it inwardly.

Very often in sport the outcome of a close match is determined by a few key points—and not so much on the outcome of those points but on *a player's reaction to those points*. When reviewing a match a player would key in on all the pivotal moments *and his emotional response* to those moments. He would get a handle on exactly where he was at, what he was thinking about, what he was feeling, and what deep-seated patterns he was repeating. If there were any emotional shifts (that led to an increase or decrease in momentum) he would become very clear about all the factors involved in that shift.

Getting clear on our emotions and deep-seated motivations is important but we want to take this a step further: more than recalling the key moments of a match we want to *positively transform these moments*. And the way to do this is to *imaginatively relive* each key moment, over and over again, until you have mastered that moment, solidified your positive mindset, and transformed every negative state into a positive one.

To give you an example: in the 2011 US Open, Golubev (who is a low-ranked player) was dominating Nadal (a top-seeded player). Golubev was ahead in *every* set but let each set slip away. The commentator said, "It's always the same script: he gets to the summit then slips, he gets to the summit then slips." Well Golubev would certainly want to change *that* script. When he reviews the match, he wants to relive his positive momentum, again and again, until he solidifies it, until he is so centered in it that nothing can shake him. Then he wants to relive every time his game went into the gutter to discover the exact mental configuration or pattern that sabotaged his game. Then he wants to replace each negative implosion with a winning mindset and an imagined victory. And he wants to do this again and again until that negative mindset is replaced by a positive one, until the subconscious substructure of defeat is replaced by one of victory, until victory and the state of victory feel natural and inevitable to him.

If Golubev loses once to Nadal on the court and wins twenty times in his imagination then, to his subconscious mind, the score would be twenty to one. That would create confidence for Golubev next time he faced a top-ranked player. [→]

But Golubev's loss over Nadal was real. Deep down he is going to know that his imagined victory was, well, imagined.

Yes—if his imagined victory is not infused with all the tones of reality. But was his loss to Nadal really real? Is it real right now? Where is Nadal? Where are the crowds? They don't exist. They are only memories. The only thing that is seemingly real is Golubev's *memory of the event*—and I'm not even sure how real that is. (It's much easier for a person to believe in the realness of his memories than in the realness of his imagined creation.) But are those mental memories any more real than his imagined revision of the match? All those memories are nothing more than recordings in his subconscious mind—and they command power over him only because he *believes they are real*. The only thing that is really real is Golubev's consciousness, his creative power, what he chooses to believe. He can believe in the realness of his memory (and his loss to Nadal) or not; he can believe in the realness of his imaginative victory or not. It's his choice. He has the power to choose the reality he wants. Whether or not he chooses to exercise that power is another matter.

Other Ways to Remove Deep-Seated Blocks

Are there any other methods we can use to remove deep-seated traumas, such as prayer or making an appeal to a higher power rather than dealing with the blocks directly?

Yes. Higher forms of prayer can certainly help clear away some of these deep-seated blocks. Prayer can also increase the positive resonance of our subconscious mind as well. *Conscious Retrieval* is the simplest method for removing or nullifying the effects of deep-seated blocks. *Creative Revision* is a step higher but it requires more trust and a higher degree of creative occupancy. Directly appealing to your higher self is another approach but this requires great trust and the clarity of intention in order to convey your intention to your higher mind. [→]

One prayer-type method to consider, which is used in the Huna tradition (the native spiritual tradition of Hawaii), is called *ho'oponopono*. This means "to make things right on every level." *Ho'oponopono* is actually a whole system of practices that is used to make things right between people but one part of this practice—which could rightly be called a prayer or an invocation—can be used to dissolve psychological blocks and "make things right" for an individual. What you do is repeat four key phrases, each of which carries a specific intention and feeling, and which can serve to raise the vibration of your whole psyche. The way to resolve a problem, a pain, a regret, or some issue you have with another person, is to hold a clear sense of the problem in your mind and *talk to the problem directly*, as if it were a friend. Approach it with love and gratitude. Don't even see it as a problem, more like an opportunity. Ask it for help. And do this by repeating the four phrases over and over, like a mantra or a positive affirmation, until the magnanimous feeling of each phrase permeates your psyche and the problem is naturally resolved. Again, the primary power does not rest in the specific words or phrasing but in the intention and feeling you bring to the words. The four phrases or invocations are:

I Admit It (or "I give myself to it"). *Admit* means "to let in" and also "to take responsibility for." Here you open to the "issue" and acknowledge that you cannot transform things on your own—through the agency of your conscious will and action—and that you need the participation of your higher mind in order to resolve this issue. Integral to your admittance is also your intention to do whatever is needed to resolve the issue and make things right. Regardless of the words you use, the intention of this phrase is to create an opening and a receptivity to both the issue at hand and your higher self. More than saying you are open you must feel open, you must be open.

Please Perfect Me (or "please make me whole," or "please enter"). This is an appeal to your higher mind to make you complete in regards to this issue, to transform and/or remove the problem and its roots, and to do what is needed to bring about a complete and beneficial resolution to the matter. Besides resolving the problem, the deeper appeal here is for the emergence of our aliveness and joy, and well-being. More than asking for perfection (or completion) you must feel it.

I Love You (or "I bring you into my heart," or "I embrace this"). This implies a total acceptance of the issue or problem, and a total trust that your higher self will resolve things in the highest and most beneficial way. To be effective you need to feel this love, this embrace, this total acceptance of the issue.

I Thank You (or "I joyfully release this," or "it is complete"). This is where you feel gratitude and appreciation—and also a sense of relief and fulfillment—for the complete and wished-for resolution of the issue. (You might also be thankful that this issue came into your life and served as a vehicle for your positive growth and transformation.) You need not wait for some kind of tangible result in order to feel thankful; knowing that everything will be accomplished exactly or better than asked for, you must revel in the feeling of joy and gratefulness now.

That "great fullness," that sense of wholeness and completion, is the ultimate goal of *ho'oponopono*. But, again, you need not wait for these sublime qualities to descend upon you in the future; you need not wait until everything is lined up in a certain way or until you reach some long-standing goal, before you feel grateful and complete. Wholeness and joy are inherent to your own nature. They're always yours. So don't wait for outer conditions to be perfect or just right, appropriate what is already yours, right now! Be the magnificence that you are, right now. *Ho'oponopono* yourself now: "I accept myself (as I am); I am whole and perfect (as I am); I love myself (all of myself, just as I am); I am thankful for this life (just as it is)." [→]

* * *

CHAPTER SEVEN:
ADOPT A WINNING MINDSET

Many players win or lose a match before they even set foot on the court—and this depends on the mindset they come with. Commenting on the first "Battle of the Sexes" tennis match played between Margaret Court and Bobby Riggs, Billy Jean King said that Court lost the match before it began—and she did so when she curtsied to Riggs after he gave her a bouquet of flowers. This indicated a mindset of acquiescence rather than one of dominance.

A winning mindset is founded upon a player's supreme confidence in himself, his innate sense of power, and his ability to play his own game regardless of what his opponent is doing or what thoughts arise in his mind. In this chapter we will explore five winning mindsets, each of which can help an athlete align with his higher mind and move toward the zone.

1. Embrace the Positive

When an athlete embraces a positive attitude, and inclines his thoughts and actions toward the positive, he puts himself in resonance with his higher self and the very nature of Life. A principle we have already stated (and one we should always bear in mind) is that *Life is purely positive*. The creative power of the universe always flows through the positive. All transformation comes by way of the positive. Aliveness and joy are always positive. We can never create anything truly beneficial or worthwhile by way of the negative.

The state of "on" can be rightly seen as the state of our higher self expressed through our developed human abilities. This state is all-encompassing and ever-victorious. It is never prompted or motivated by fear or loss but always by the true and positive qualities of life. Positivity, aliveness, and joy are integral to the state of "on."

Never Give In to Negative Emotions

One key to positive power is to never give in to doubt, fear, or negative emotions. Never entertain these inner enemies; never afford them any of your attention; never let them determine your actions or your state of consciousness; never let them usurp your power. Should these enemies raise their ugly heads never accept them, never identify with them, never believe in them. Don't even give them enough attention to then try and get rid of them. Don't react to them. Don't afford them one moment of existence. A champion has nothing to do with such diseases. You should have nothing to do with them either.

The Super-Positive

More than adopting a positive mindset we want to enter the realm of the *super-positive*. We want to embrace the sheer exuberance of Life. More than winning a game or a contest we want to win the splendor of our own being. We want to feel the thrill of playing our game to perfection, of being unified in body, mind, and spirit, of having our inner mastery express itself as outer victory. And we can do this when we stand in our own greatness; when we unify ourselves with the splendor of our own nature. This also puts our entire psyche in resonance with the ever-positive, ever-victorious power of the universe. And as they say in Aikido: "If you become one (in mind and heart) with the universe, your opponent must defeat the whole universe in order to defeat you." Now that's a pretty tall order!

2. Don't Play Against an "Opponent"—Play Your Game

> The competitor who is motivated by pride or greed, or interested primarily in defeating an opponent, will go weak at the moment of the starting gun and be unable to achieve the maximum continued effort necessary for great achievement.
> (Hawkins, *Power vs Force*, p. 175)

When an athlete adopts a mindset based upon personal mastery and excellence—and not upon the need to be better than someone else or prove oneself to others—he moves out of his primitive fight-or-flight mode toward the state of his higher self. As a general rule, we want our actions to be motivated by that which is positive and life-inspiring. We never want our actions to be based upon negative or "low vibration" states such as fear, selfishness, or indecision; or upon the petty satisfaction that might come from beating someone else. These "low" motivational states are at odds with our ever-positive nature and never lead to lasting gains or real transformation.

One emotion we never want as our prime motivating factor is fear. Fear disjoints our mind-body connection and hampers our game, especially at higher levels of play. Also, when we fear something we unconsciously impart it with a certain degree of power over us; we allow it to take up a large portion of our awareness and life-energy. And recall that whatever we are aware of, whatever we focus on, we expand and enliven. So, if you fear an opponent (or something inside yourself) you have already lost the first battle—you have given him the mainstay of your attention and shifted the center of your power away from yourself and unto him.

Here's another rule to keep in mind: we never want the person we're playing against to determine our thoughts or our actions. We never want our focus to be on our opponent or on him losing; rather we always want it to be on the highest in ourselves and on our victory. When working on the mental game, and life itself it's important to understand that your higher self *only sees what you provide it with*, what you hold true in *your* mind—whether you are conscious of it or not. So, if you wish for something bad to happen to your opponent—such as that he miss his serve or lose the point—your subconscious mind picks up the negative vibration of that thought and "miss the serve" or "lose the point" gets registered *for you*. Whatever we wish on others is the very thing that *we* get because *we* created the wish; *we* are holding the wish in our mind and in our heart.

Another thing to bear in mind is that your higher mind *only conceives what it wants*—and it holds the same to be true for you. It assumes that you only conceive, and think about, what you want. If you embrace a particular thought or belief, or hold something in your awareness, your higher mind operates upon the premise that that is something you want. If you did not want it, why on earth would you hold it in your awareness? So, if you hold something in your awareness (which means that it's something you want) your higher mind endeavors to produce it for you. Accordingly, whatever you hold in your awareness (or believe deep-down) becomes a directive to you higher mind to produce that very thing for your. Knowing this, you have to be vigilant and careful about what you focus on and what you hold in your mind (and heart) because that is what you will get. If you view your opponent or some future outcome with fear you'll get more of *your* fear. If you doubt yourself, you'll get more of *your* doubt. If you hope your opponent will lose you'll get things in resonance with loss. The same applies to all your positive feelings as well. Your task, then, is to hold in your mind and heart that which you positively want because that is what you'll get more of now and in the future.

I'm sure you've heard the expression, "Those who judge shall be judged." Well, this has nothing to do with some higher power lording over you, and judging you for judging others, and then meting out some kind of punishment. It has to do with your power and what you choose to create for yourself.

As stated, your higher mind only registers *your* thoughts and feelings; it cannot distinguish between the thoughts and feelings you have for yourself and those you have for others. To your higher mind every mental state that *you have* is something you created and is something you want. If you focus on the faults of others (or yourself), if you have negative feelings toward others (or yourself), that's what gets communicated to your subconscious mind and that is what *you* get more of. If you judge others, you get the negativity of that judgment. It's as simple as that.

Let's also consider the positive mode: "Those who love will be loved." As before, you will not receive love from some Higher Power as a reward for loving others; your own love for others will be picked up by your higher mind and be redoubled for you. And that love will not only harmonize your whole being it will put you in perfect accord with the all of Life.

> To think feelingly on any state impresses it on the subconscious. Therefore, if you dwell on difficulties, barriers, or delay, the subconscious, by its very non-selective nature, accepts the feeling of difficulty and obstacles as your request and proceeds to produce them in your outer world.
> (Goddard, *The Neville Reader*, p. 173)

3. *Play with Effortlessness and Ease*

> The less tension and effort, the faster and more powerful you will be. ~Bruce Lee

A primary aim of every higher athlete should be to get in touch with his innate sense of effortlessness and ease. Ease puts us in resonance with our higher mind; and when we are in resonance with our higher mind it brings power, ease, and consistency to our game. If a player grunts and groans, and tries real hard with every shot, he may want to re-think this approach. Though this overt kind of effort may help pump up some players it's not likely to deliver the goods at the highest level of play (where both power and gracefulness are needed). When we look at tennis, and Novak Djokovic's game (especially during the time when he was virtually unbeatable), we can see this perfect blend of ease and power. A player whose game is founded upon ease and power is a step ahead of one who relies solely on power and exertion.

When working on a shot, when hitting the ball, what are you focused on? Where are you in the shot? Most players are in the domain of their cognitive mind—concentrating, trying real hard, employing techniques. But what about naturalness and ease? Where's that? That's where you want to be centered. You can hit the ball as hard as you like but *hit from a place of naturalness and ease.* Don't focus too much on personal will as this may forestall the invincible power of your higher self from entering your game. Be at ease; go with the flow.

Nothing to Lose

I'm sure you've heard the expression, "He's got nothing to lose." When a player has nothing to lose, when the pressure is off, such as when he's down in the match (and lets go of the hope of victory) he can finally let go and begin to play with ease. And guess what happens? Things start to turn around. He loosens up; his shots are not so tight. He starts to play a lot better. So why wait until you have nothing to lose? Why not relax and bring in that state of ease from the beginning?

With all this emphasis on mental toughness, giving it your all, huffing and puffing and blowing the house down, this "soft" quality of ease is often overlooked. As a higher athlete, as a student of the higher game, we don't want to make this mistake: we want naturalness and ease—along with its conjunctives of joy, aliveness, power, and beauty—to be the foundation of every shot, every game, and every dimension of life. Ease is a quality of our higher mind and integral to the state of "on"—so don't leave home, or take your shot, without it.

4. Enjoy the Game

We hear it all the time: "Do what you love." When you do what you love—and to a lesser extent when you think about what you love—you open yourself to the inherent joy of Life. But we don't have to be told to do what we love because this is already our natural inclination. All we need do is to do it! Doing what we love and doing it with all our heart aligns us with the luminous flow of life and the state of "on." So it's quite helpful, at every level of play, to get in touch with your heart, your love, and the inherent joy of life itself.

Very often, when a top player is asked about his strategy for an upcoming game, he says, "I'm just going to go out there and enjoy myself." If you can enjoy yourself, if you can embody your inherent sense of aliveness and joy, you can toss away all the methods and just play your game. The bottom line is this: find your joy, revel in your aliveness, expand the love and fullness of your own nature. This is the gateway that opens you to the state of "on." All the rest is commentary.

5. Adopt the Mindset of a Champion

> I believe that a champion wins in his mind first and then plays the game—not the other way around. ~Alex Rodriguez

The mindset of a champion is marked by clarity, presence, and supreme confidence. Every time a champion steps onto the court or the playing field he fully expects to win; and even when he's down he still expects to win. More than expecting to win, he views it as an inevitability, as the way things are meant to be. It is this mindset of certainty; this is the unflinching belief in oneself that delivers an athlete to his highest game and makes him an inner and outer champion.

Certainty

Certainty is a particular mode of consciousness that is different from ordinary thought; it is a mode of consciousness that unites us with the creative power of the universe. It's a state of singularity, of being "all in"; it's a state where our power is not undermined (or nullified) by the countercurrents of fear, hesitation, or doubt.

When Spirit creates this universe, it does so with certainty and singularity of intent. It is never divided or at odds with its own creative expression; it is never in a state of uncertainty or doubt where it wants one thing but at the same time believes something else to be true. (Animals are never divided against themselves either; only human beings are capable of that!) In this mode of certainty and singularity the creative power of Spirit is never thwarted or diminished. Whatever Spirit conceives comes to fruition because there is nothing in the universe that opposes it. (And, since it always gets what it conceives, it only conceives that which it wants). Although a person can never reach this supreme level of creative power, when he acts from a state of certainty he comes into resonance with Spirit, he dispels fear and doubt, he infuses his thoughts and actions with conviction, power, and inevitability.

Certainty is the mindset we want to have when we step onto the playing field or begin any worthwhile endeavor. And this mindset can only come about when we have supreme confidence and an unshakable conviction in ourselves; when we are in touch with our own power and the highest good of Spirit; when we are not plagued by doubt or fear, and have what it takes to go "all in."

When we're certain about victory, that certainty becomes a potent force that helps lead us to that eventuality. If we hope something is going to happen, that's good; if we are confident something is going to happen, that's better; but if we *know* something is going to happen, that knowingness activates our higher mind and infuses our actions with its power. That's the mindset we want to adopt and bring with us to every game.

> Thought, in reality, is none other than pure consciousness. Even so, it serves as a means to liberation [and creative power] for the individual only when it takes the form of certainty. ~Abhinavagupta (10th Century Kashmiri sage)

The Bhav of a Champion

When I was living at an ashram in India I chanted and meditated a lot. I also learned many Sanskrit words. One word I heard quite often was *bhav*. A person's *bhav* is the way he holds himself; the position or attitude he has; his "feel" or presence. So, we want the *bhav* of a champion; we want the *feel* of a champion, the aura of a champion, the posture of a champion, the walk and talk of a champion. Every time we enter a game or a match we want to walk in like we own the place. We want victory to feel perfectly natural to us, like our birthright. This is something more than role-playing, where we imagine ourselves to be a great player or a champion: this is where we fully assume the role of a champion, where we embody the feel or *bhav* of a champion. This mindset, this state of embodiment, is what draws our highest potential and the inevitability of victory. This is the mindset we want to hold all the time; this is the mindset that transforms an athlete into a champion.

CHAPTER EIGHT:
MEDITATE (ACCESS THE CORE OF YOUR BEING)

People have a lot of thoughts *about* life and they are ever *reacting* to the conditions of life but rarely do they have a direct experience of life itself. And that is because they live through their thoughts and emotions and not their own presence. So what to do? How do we get in touch with life itself and our true nature? How do get out of our mentalized version of life and experience the joy of our being, the core of our existence?

Most people are not even concerned with discovering their own nature; and that's because they have no real sense that it's missing. Their primary concern is with various pursuits—such as attaining wealth, finding relationships, winning at this or that, working on projects, etc.—in the hopes that all this will bring them happiness. And, to some extent, it does. Yet it never brings the true prize or lasting fulfillment. Some people take this pursuit inward and work with their mind, trying to stop their thoughts in the hope that this will bring them some peace. Others use affirmations and creative visualizations, hoping this will improve their condition and attract abundance into their lives. And all of these things can be helpful and are often a good first step but they cannot truly satisfy the longing of one's heart or soul. The only way to do that is to realize your own nature and your direct connection to Life. Meditation (which includes other practices like the practice of presence) can help with this. Meditation is the primary means by which a person can get beyond the prison of his mind, abide in the splendor of his own nature, and partake more fully in the wonder of Life.

Meditation

I've been involved with meditation and the path of enlightenment for over thirty years. I've studied numerous spiritual disciplines and spent years meditating in Zen monasteries and yogic ashrams. While living at an ashram in India, I would wake up every morning at 3:00 a.m., meditate for two hours, chant for an hour and a half, run to a nearby temple (about two miles down the road), make an offering, and then return to begin my day of selfless service. I've written about spiritual practice and have taught meditation in various places throughout the world. And what I've learned is that there is no real mystery to any of this; meditation is our natural state. It is something very simple. You need not pack up your stuff and move to an ashram or a Buddhist monastery in order to meditate. You need not read a lot of books on the subject either. You can meditate in a deep and natural way without any of that. And though the practice of meditation is simple it's not easy—at least not in the beginning. What you need is precise instructions, a firm yet flexible mind, and sincerity of effort. Having a good meditation instructor may also be necessary.

Meditation is the conscious abidance in your own nature. It is something very simple and natural but usually misunderstood and overlooked. That's because most people live in their mind (and its version of reality) while being aloof to their own self. To apperceive the state of meditation we must break free of our habitual reliance on the mind and employ a very subtle mode of awareness. We must fine-tune our intuition and sensitivity; we must come into a new relationship with our own self; we must be willing to stand firm in who we are and not allow every thought and emotion to pull us from our true center.

Virtually all of our time—from the moment we wake up till the time we fall asleep—is spent in our mind and its world of thought. Our life is comprised of thoughts, reactions, concerns, emotions, etc. but not our true self. We have no center, no stable foundation. In meditation our aim is to shift the nexus of our awareness and *the very place from where we live our lives* from an unconscious abidance in thought to a conscious abidance in presence, from our thoughts *about* life to life itself.

To meditate, to consciously abide in your own presence, you must first get beyond the inertial pull of your subconscious mind. To do this you must empower your conscious mind and develop your powers of will and concentration. You need a mind that is strong and able to keep its attention on one thing for an extended period of time; but you don't want a mind that is too strong or too concretized (because then your focus becomes too narrow). You want a mind that is firm yet open, spacious and translucent; you want to be in a state of "relaxed concentration." This state opens you to meditation and higher levels of awareness. And this, as you may recognize, is also the state that leads an athlete toward the state of "on."

Many people in this MTV, Twitter world find it difficult to hold a single focus for a sustained period of time. I recall when I first started meditating at the San Francisco Zen Center; the basic practice was to follow the breath, counting from *one* to *ten*. This seemed easy enough but before I could reach a count of *five* my mind would wander off somewhere. A few minutes later, when I realized I was lost in thought, I would bring myself back to the present moment and start again. Try as I may, for the first week or so I kept getting derailed before I could reach *ten*. This is what it means to be in the fog of the subconscious mind. Looking back now, it seems impossible that I was so easily distracted; however, this is the state that many people are in. So the first step is to develop focus and attention and to rise above the relentless pull of the subconscious mind. This is where a lot of work is needed, especially at the beginning. Being able to focus on a single object for a sustained period of time is not meditation but a prelude to it. Athletes who have cultivated their powers of concentration and are able to hold a steady focus will be one step closer to meditation than people who are wholly lost in their stream of thought.

Meditation versus Meditation Methods

It's important to bear in mind that the *state of meditation* (which is the conscious abidance in one's own nature, beyond the mind) is something different from *methods of meditation*, which are artful employments of the mind. These methods can be understood as forms of concentration or mind-stabilizing techniques that can help someone appease the restlessness of his mind and bring about a state that is more present, focused, and relaxed. These methods are also designed to uplift our consciousness and provide the right resonance for meditation but they should not be confused with meditation itself. True meditation is beyond all methods; it's simply the state of abidance in your own nature, beyond the mind and thought.

Most meditation methods entail some form of concentration but they are more than mere focus techniques; they usually involve a sacred object, a feeling of reverence, use of the breath, and concentration on various energy centers. This kind of reverent one-pointedness raises the vibration of our psyche, opens our heart, and puts our mind in resonance with our higher self and the state of meditation.

Common meditation methods include being aware of the breath, repeating a sacred phrase or mantra (such as the words "I am"), or holding your attention on a sacred object, such as a flame, a deity, a guru, a word, or a geometric pattern. They can also include concentrating on various locations in the body (such as the heart or lower belly region) or on some sacred sound such as *om* or *hu*; or involve witnessing your thoughts with complete detachment, just letting them pass like clouds passing through the sky. More advanced methods include focusing on the space between the breathing in and the breathing out or on pure awareness itself. Simpler methods, which are more or less relaxation techniques, include listening to peaceful music or sitting in nature. There are also different forms of prayer, which many people associate with meditation; and also creative visualizations and affirmations that can be seen as positive uses of the mind (but not meditation itself). As you can see the list of methods is quite long, yet I do not speak of these as a mere observer—I have practiced all of these methods.

Each meditation method reaches its culmination when you become aware of the one who is aware; when you become aware of the one who is following the method; when you become established in the immovable presence of your own being. If you're focused on a sacred word and come to sense the one who is aware of the word, stop concentrating on the word and stay with that presence, with that ever-present consciousness that is prior to thought. The same holds true for any object of concentration: when the method has delivered you beyond the mind to a direct sense of your own presence, let go of the method and stay with your presence. Station yourself there. Feel into and *become* that presence, that all-embracing consciousness that you already are. That's the heart of meditation.

Simple Meditation Instructions

Formal meditation is usually carried out in a sitting position, either on a firm cushion (placed on a mat or a carpeted floor) or on a chair (with your feet resting firmly on the floor). It's important to sit with your back straight and be in an upright, alert position. Your posture should be firm yet flexible, stable yet soft. Your hands can be placed on your lap or anywhere that is comfortable. Assuming this balanced, steady posture places your body in resonance with the qualities of your higher self.

You can meditate with your eyes open (where you see what is in front of you but are not focused on anything in particular) or with your eyes closed. When your eyes are closed the subconscious mind has more power over your awareness and you are more likely to drift off into a semi-conscious, dreamlike state, especially at the beginning. So, if you have a tendency to get lost in thought (or fall into a subconscious slumber) you may want to start out with your eyes open.

Ideally, the environment should be serene and quiet; if, however, there is some noise that's alright. Just don't get involved with it or let it distract you. A little noise can be helpful as this may prevent you from drifting off. A good start is to meditate twice a day, in the morning and evening, for about twenty minutes.

A simple way to begin meditation practice is by focusing on the breath in the lower belly region. Focusing on the breath in this area provides stability and energetic grounding. If you like, you can count from *one* to *ten* with each breath but it's better to just follow the breath without counting, being keenly aware of the in-breath and the out-breath and the feel of each breath. If your mind wanders off somewhere gently, and without any kind of self-criticism, bring it back to the breath. Drifting off into a dreamlike state can be very relaxing but it's not meditation; it's not going to help you deepen your sense of presence.

Awareness of the breath is a good mind-stabilizing technique and a prelude to meditation. In order to move into a true state of meditative awareness you must shift your focus to a more subtle and rarefied dimension of your being—to the consciousness, or "I"-ness, or conscious presence that is aware of the breath. Who is aware of the breath? See if you can get a clear sense of that aware-presence, that subjective experiencer (which is often felt in the center or toward the back of the head). If you can sense or feel that conscious self then let go of your focus on the breath and stay with that presence, that pure awareness. That is where you want to abide.

Another kind of meditation method involves being aware of your thoughts (and, later, sensing the one who is aware of your thoughts). The virtue of this method is that it can help create some distance between you, the conscious subject, and the thoughts you are watching. This can help break *your habitual and unconscious identification with thought.* Another approach is to repeat a word or phrase and the feeling it evokes. (In Eastern meditative traditions a sacred word or phrase that is repeated again and again is called a *mantra*.) A simple method is to inwardly repeat the words, "I am." It's always beneficial to coordinate the words with the breath. So, you would repeat the words "I am" on the in-breath and "I am" on the out-breath; or "I" on the in-breath and "am" on the out-breath. Once you're able to hold a steady focus on the words "I am" go deeper and see if you can sense the actual feel of the words and get a clear sense of your own existence or beingness. You can use any positive phrase as a mantra, such as "I am the power and the glory" or "Everything is perfection." The exact phrase does not matter; what matters is the positive feeling evoked by the words and the way the words can appease your mind and lead you toward an awareness of the pure sense of "I am," the pure sense of your own existence.

When using a self-styled mantra be careful not to use any kind of double-negative phrase or some phrase that assumes a negative condition you want to overcome. For example, you make think that the phrase "no fear, no fear" has a positive meaning but it will not register that way with your subconscious mind. Your subconscious mind may hear and respond to the words separately; it may hear two negative words—"no" and "fear"—rather than the positive phrase you intended.

Another method you can use is to become aware of the breath in the lower belly or heart region and then attune to *the space or gap between the breaths*. When you become aware of this gap or nothingness between the breaths (which is not something your mind can grab hold of) you may reach a moment of stillness where your mind suddenly stops and opens to pure awareness. So long as the mind is focused on an object—which could be a thought, a mantra, an energy center, the breath, etc.—it remains in control of your experience. Only when it breaks free of this object-based focus and *stops* and *opens* (and gets out of the way) does it allow for the emergence of a higher presence or pure awareness. Abidance in our own nature as pure, objectless awareness is the heart of meditation.

When you reach the state of presence, or pure "I"-ness, just remain there. Let that presence expand and infuse your being with a beneficent sense of well-being. Using the power of the breath may help stabilize the state; so, whenever there is a "wobble" in your focus or a sidetrack into the subconscious undertow of thought gently bring your awareness back to your breath, back to the here and now. Ultimately this is not about being *aware of* your own presence but *knowing it directly*—and the only way to know it directly is to be it. [→]

With these methods we're trying to reach a state of repose by pulling ourselves out of the mire and madness of the mind. (Said another way, we're trying to get away from Thought Dude and into the room with Presence Dude.) But your mind may not want to do this and so your thoughts might get more and more chaotic and loud. (For sure, Thought Dude is gonna start screaming and throwing fits.) So, instead of getting into a state of repose with these meditation methods a beginner might find himself more entangled with his own mind. Frustration may result. To help remedy this, it's helpful to meditate in a group or with the help of a teacher.

Three-fold Awareness Practice

Before trying to formally meditate I would recommend using a method that involves holding three things in your awareness at the same time. (I first heard about this method from Ezra Bayda of the Los Angeles Zen Center; he also discusses this method in his book, *Zen Heart*.) The practice is to simultaneously hold an awareness of a) your breath, b) your body-sense, which is the *felt* sense you have of your own body, and c) your surroundings, which usually includes what you see or hear. As you hold an awareness of these three things, *at the same time*, your cognitive agency is so occupied that it has no room left to think, no room left to offer its usual commentary, no power to control things and then, quite spontaneously, the presence of your higher self may emerge. This is essentially what takes place in the state of "on" as well. The cognitive mind is sidetracked; its grip on your awareness is softened and a higher dimension of self is able to shine through. Something else may be going on as well. Your cognitive mind is linear; it cannot truly focus on more than one thing at a time. So, when you're prompted to be aware of three things at the same time your cognitive mind will keep trying to do this for you but without success; and so, at some point, you will have to access your higher mind or intuitive mind in order to accomplish this.

This three-fold practice is simply but not so easy. You will have to practice it over and over again. First, you have to get a clear sense of your breath, and establish your awareness there, before you can become aware of your body and your body sense. You may keep losing one or both foci of awareness, and that's okay. Just come back to the breath; see if you can establish your awareness there; and then, holding that, become aware of your body. When you're able to hold both foci simultaneously, become aware of your environment. The mind will always put up its resistance, so you must practice. Take a walk, and practice. Whenever you have some free time, practice.

The reason one should begin with this method (or use it while also practicing formal meditation) is that meditation is the abidance in your own presence—if, however, you have no sense of your own presence, and have never accessed it, abiding there will not be possible. You will sit for meditation and be wrestling with your monkey-mind the whole time. This is not what you want. You can practice this three-fold method while taking a walk around the block, when you first wake up, when you lay down to go to sleep, or any time you're free. And you don't have to follow any strict rules. You can try to focus on your body, then the breath, then the environment. It might also be helpful to add a mantra to the breath, such as repeating "I" on the in-breath and "am" on the outbreath. Keep practicing. You should be able to master this practice in a short amount of time. After you have established this practice you're likely to become aware of your breath and/or your presence naturally, throughout the day, without using any method. You'll also be able to evoke your presence, the constant of your own being, at will, when needed.

The Constant of Presence

Earlier we spoke about constants, which are immovable reference-points that an athlete can come back to again and again to help stabilize his mind, his game, and his life. The main constant we explored was conscious breathing and an awareness of the breath. However, there is one constant that is even more fundamental than the breath or anything you can focus on with your mind and that's the constant of your own being, your own presence. In every game you play, in every shot you take, in every experience you have there is one thing that is always present and the same—and that is you. *You are the constant.* Your presence is the constant. Your sense of your own self and your own beingness is the constant. It's always present yet this immovable constant is always overlooked. The way to make this every-present constant the anchor of your life *is by being aware of it,* by consciously being who you already are. You are that pure presence beyond the mind, beyond all the thoughts that are telling you who you are. Don't get tricked into thinking you are every thought—you are something much greater than thought. So station your life and your awareness there, where you really are. Don't be the thoughts you have about yourself—be yourself!

> Most people fret about losing this state or that state. They get caught up in what's not present anymore. . . . What *haven't* you lost? That is what's important. What always is? What is there in bliss and misery [in good thoughts and bad]? Who you are is always present and is always the same. You are that permanence that contains all becoming and be-going. That which doesn't come and go is real. That is where freedom is found—nowhere else.
> (Adyashanti, *The Impact of Awakening,* p. 31)

──────── ℛ∘ℛ∘ℛ∘ℛ ────────

What is the relationship between the state of presence and the zone? Does the practice of presence move us toward the zone or incline us in that direction?

The zone and our true presence both relate to our higher mind, to a state of pure consciousness beyond the distractions of our cognitive mind. Presence can be seen as a state of the higher mind when not engaged in a particular action, while the state of "on" can be seen as a state of the higher mind when expressed through our skills and actions. All said, the more we come in contact with the state of our higher mind (when at rest) through an apperception of our own presence, the more we incline ourselves toward the zone in sport and in life.

I heard that when working on ourselves or any kind of mental mastery that it's important to keep good company. What exactly is good company?

The words and attitudes of others can have a huge impact on your inner state and your life so, yes, you want to keep good company. You want to be around people who make you feel supported, uplifted, and empowered, people who inspire you. You don't want to be around people who make you feel down and uninspired.

Sometimes we don't have a choice and negative people come into our lives. Yet how we respond to those people, how deeply we let them affect us is within our realm of choice. Instead of resisting everything and asking "why me?" you may want to make a shift and ask, "What can I learn from this?"

More important than keeping good company outwardly (in terms of people) is to keep good company inwardly, to "hang out with" positive and uplifting thoughts, to orient yourself toward positive feelings while staying away from fear, self-doubt, self-loathing, and all the rest. If a negative thought arises let it arise but don't meet it with more negativity; simply observe it from a state of centeredness and higher awareness. Get in touch with the infinite consciousness that is aware of the negative thought, and hang out there, not in the negative thought itself. Keep the company of yourself as that pure, all-embracing awareness. That is best good company you can ever have. [→]

A Final Thought

There's a principle we have spoken about again and again and it is this: what we focus on, where we choose to place our awareness, is where we are. And, over time, this becomes *who* we are. When we focus on all the small stuff around us, when we're all wrapped up in our mental chatter and our ever-revolving concerns, that is where we are, that is the world we come to live in. When we focus on the grand things, on our true essence, on our ideals, on our own presence, that is where we are, that is the world we create for ourselves. And what we focus on—and, thus, the future we create for ourselves—is determined by us, by our choice.

We, as human beings, have forgotten that we occupy the creative center of our own lives. We consider all the things we want to do or attain but never who we really are, our essence. We live in a world where the most important thing is missing—and that is our own self, our inherent unity with life. Worse still, we unwittingly use our vast creative power to construct a life of pain and limitations rather than one of freedom, joy, and limitless possibilities.

The right use of our intelligence, consciousness, and creative power is the means by which we can effectuate a positive change in our life and bring about a true sense of purpose and value. The fundamental change we want to make is to move beyond our identification with thought; to expand our innate sense of aliveness and joy; and to become aware of the core of our being. Thoughts come and go, games are won and lost, but the glory of our own self ever-remains. Our true self is the ultimate constant. It is the source of all peace, the essence of all power, the gateway to all of life's wonder.

Book Two

Questions & Answers

QUESTIONS & ANSWERS I
THE STATE OF "ON"

The Zone and the State of "On"

You've been using the term "on" as opposed the more common term, "the zone" or "the flow." Is there any appreciable difference between the state of "on" and the zone?

The zone, the flow, and the state of "on" all point to the same exalted state where an athlete is not just playing well or to the best of his abilities but where he enters a higher dimension of self and plays beyond anything he normally believes himself capable of. Being in the zone generally refers to a state where everything is going right, where you are playing really well, where there is a certain ease and flow to your game. When this happens to an athlete you often hear a sports commentator say something like, "He's in the zone." Being in the state of "on" is pretty much the same thing but I see it as involving a deeper level of our existence.

I've played sports all my life and, perhaps due to my natural talent and overall positive outlook on life, I would often reach an exalted level of play. But the first time I encountered the state of "on" it was something quite different from playing well. It felt as if I was "on fire," and "on my game" and "on target"—but there was something more. Everything took place as I intended. My shots hit their mark. And sometimes, without having a specific intention, by just putting forth a feeling, things would happen in some unexpected way. Afterwards, when describing this state to a friend, I kept saying, "I was on." And so I called it "on" or the state of "on." In terms of terms, however, being in the zone, in the flow, or in the state of "on" all point to the same state of exalted skill in action, a state not only empowered by your own skill but by your higher mind as well.

Concentration

Being in the state of "on" (or in the zone) is often associated with focus and concentration. How important is this, and is it possible to focus too much?

Focus is needed to overcome mental distractions and the undertow of our subconscious thoughts yet when our focus is too rigid and too commanding of our attention (and when we rely too much on our cognitive focus) we get cut off from the animating power of our higher mind. There's an art to this. It's not about having an unyielding or steely focus; it's about having enough focus to get beyond the distractedness of the cognitive mind but then being able to "let go" and open up to the operation of your higher mind. Too little or too much focus is not going to get you there; you have to go right down the middle. It's a bit like holding a carving tool: if you hold it too firmly or too loosely you will not have full control over it.

> Without realizing it, I had stumbled onto the coexistence of opposites—rest and alertness, composure and vigorous exercise—the formula for the Zone.
> (Douillard, *Body, Mind, and Sport*, p. 230)

What are some of the primary obstacles to reaching the zone?

A primary obstacle is that the grip of one's cognitive mind is too tight, that it commands too much attention. Most people rely upon that mind way too much. They live in a world of thought, in exile from their higher self, and miles away from the zone. Another obstacle—and a prime reason why so few people are able to access the zone—is that they are completely out of touch with their inherent sense of aliveness and joy, which is the very nature of the zone. In addition, most people are just not sensitized to the subtle operation of their higher mind and so they miss it even when it's in their midst. Few athletes are able to reach the zone because most have been conditioned to miss it. Most athletes don't access the zone because they don't know what steps to take or they're nor willing to do the groundwork that's required. To play well you have to practice. To access the zone you have to practice. There's no magical pill you can take to get you there. You have to do the work.

Imagination

> I never hit a shot, even in practice, without having a very sharp, in-focus picture of it in my head.   ~Jack Nicklaus [→]

What about visualizing a shot and practicing it in our imagination? Is this useful?

It can be very useful, especially for a player who wants to improve his focus and imaginative powers. Practicing a shot in your imagination also creates a neural pattern in the brain similar to one created by real-life practice; and studies indicate that a combination of real-life practice along with imaginary practice is more effective than real-life practice alone.

When I was living in an ashram in India, doing my best to reach the supreme state of enlightenment, each morning I would meditate for about two hours each morning, have some tea, called *chai*, then chant for about an hour and a half. At the end of this long chant, during a repetitive, melodic section I would often perform a mental worship of the deity. I would imagine a beautiful setting with fruit, gems, and flowers, and all kinds of divine beings. Now many people do physical worship, such as all the people who go to church or temple, but you never know what they're thinking about. A person could go through an entire Sunday service yet all the while be thinking about his usual concerns. Not so with mental worship. If you're not fully present the entire scene disappears. But being fully conscious is only half the story: in addition to this you must enter the realness of the scene you have imagined. You must feel devotion and respond to the scene as if it were occurring in real life. Without this, the whole thing is lifeless and inert.

And what does this have to with practicing shots in your imagination? Well, with imaginary practice you have to be 100% present else the whole scene disappears. Moreover, it's not enough to simply hit the ball in your imagination—to have real effectiveness you must impart your imagined shot with all the feel and tonality of a physical shot. And the more fully you respond to your imagined shot as being real (feeling really good when you hit your shot exactly as intended) the faster it's going to get picked up by your subconscious mind and the faster you're going to gain mastery over it.

The key to success in this endeavor is to enter and feel and respond to the imagined scene as if it were a real-life reality; and to repeat this over and over again until it feels perfectly natural to you, until it becomes a lived reality.

Knowingness and Intuition

> At that special level, all sorts of odd things happened. . . . It was almost as if we were playing in slow motion. During those spells I could almost sense how the next play would develop and where the next shot would be taken.
> (Bill Russell, *Second Wind*)

Some athletes describe the state of "on" as one of extrasensory perception, where they're able to perceive things beyond the normal reach of the senses. How is this possible?

"On" is a state of heightened intuition which, from our normal perspective, may *seem* like a state of extrasensory perception. As already mentioned, human beings have two minds:

a conscious mind (that perceives through the senses, in a linear fashion) and a super-conscious mind (that perceives intuitively and instantaneously). When you get in touch with your higher mind there's an immediate knowingness; you perceive everything in an instant; and in this state you *do* have an extra sense, so to speak. You can't read a number off a card you cannot see—well, maybe you can—but this is not the kind of extra perception we're interested in.

How is it that time itself seems to slow down?

What slows down is "sensorial" time or "psychological" time. In the state of "on" we have a new relationship to the passage of time. We don't need to think about everything in order to understand it, as we do with our conscious mind. So it's not that time slows down it's more that our ability to take in and read incoming information speeds up.

Using an example from baseball, a batter may be facing a great closer in the bottom of the ninth, and he may be ready for a classic cutter or a fastball. He is concentrating on the pitcher, the ball, or something specific to the action; but all the while, even though he's not aware of it, his higher mind is taking in everything, including all the visual and auditory cues that his cognitive mind is missing. His higher mind senses the subtle changes in the pitcher's positioning that broadcasts the pitch before the ball is released. Every pitcher sends a signal, no matter how slight, as to the exact pitch he's going to throw before he throws it. Our cognitive mind is not sensitive enough to read the "tell" but our higher mind is. When you're in the realm of your higher mind you have a lot more time than when you're locked into your normal perceptual mode. And in this state a really fast fastball may look pretty slow.

Does attuning to our intuition or becoming more sensitive to the subtleties of life also attune us to the state of "on"?

Yes. And your question is well-stated: we become attuned to the state of "on" when we attune to the higher dimensions of our own self. Bear in mind that life, our own nature, and the state of "on" are conjunct, meaning they always show up together, you cannot have one without having them all. So, as we move closer to the core of life, and our higher self, we always move closer to the state of "on."

Creativity

You mentioned that the state of "on" was not a passive state but one that was creative and expressive. Could you explain?

The state of "on" does not just happen to you; you bring it about whether you're aware of it or not. On one level or another you are creating it. It may seem as if this state descends upon you from on high yet, unbeknownst to you, you are creating it through the agency of your higher self. It may seem as if the state is coming out of nowhere but that's only because you are not aware of the power within you that's giving rise to it.

Many people describe this as a state where they think something is going to happen and it happens. Is this a state of clairvoyance or being able to know the future?

> During those spells I could almost sense how the next play would develop and where the next shot would be taken. Even before the other team brought the ball in bounds, I could feel it so keenly that I'd want to shout to my teammates, "It's coming there!"—except that I knew everything would change if I did. My premonitions would be consistently correct.
> (Bill Russell, *Second Wind*)

This seeming clairvoyance is usually the result of an increased sensitivity and a more profound attunement to what is happening around you. When we are operating from our intuitive mind, which is a lot faster than our cognitive mind, things seem to slow down so much that we may feel as if we know things before they happen. This may be due to a higher attunement, a quicker reading of the cues and tells; and since you're unfamiliar with this heightened state it seems as if you can tell things before they happen. But there might be another explanation as well. The state of "on" is, as mentioned, *a creative state*; it's a state where we are unified with the Creative Power of the Universe. We know what's going to happen because, on one level, *we are creating it*. This truth was reflected in a fortune cookie I got in Kingston, New York, which read, "The best way to know the future is to create it."

I like a good Tommy Lee Jones movie now and again. At the end of *Men in Black II* we learn that an intergalactic queen had been living in New York City, working at a pizza parlor, and all the while believing she was an ordinary human being. She tells "Agent K" (Tommy Lee Jones) that she is just like everyone else—she cries because it rains. To which he replies, "You don't cry because it rains, baby, it rains because you cry." She was a galactic queen, *causing* it to rain by her sadness, yet she was not aware of it. This, too, is our situation: we, as human beings, are always one with the primary cause of our own lives yet we are not aware of this. We are only aware of the part of our self that reacts to everything, not the part that is actually creating it. However, when we're "on" something shifts: we move into ownership of our creative power; we sense ourselves at the joyous center of creation even though we may not fully realize what it is or from where it originates.

> You are creating your destiny every moment, *whether you know it or not*. Much that is good and even wonderful has come into your life without your having any inkling that you were the creator of it. (Neville, *Power of Awareness*, p. 119)

Harmonization

I see the state of "on" as one where our body, mind, and psyche all come together in perfect harmony. Is this the case?

Yes, that's one way to describe it. This harmonization of body, mind, and spirit brings about a greater flow of life-energy and affords us greater access to our own aliveness and power. In our normal state we're always contracted and divided against ourselves; there's a lot of noise and interference going on. This makes us less effective. This disrupts the harmony and flow between our body, mind, and spirit. However, when we're "on" every dimension of self supports and informs the other; there's no sense of being at odds with oneself; there's a perfect flow and "translation" between body, mind, and spirit

A Higher Unifying Principle

Every quality inherent to our true nature—such as love, aliveness, and euphoria—can be seen as a "higher unifying principle" in that the experience (and emotive power) of this quality naturally unifies our whole being. For instance, when we make a good shot and feel excited that excitement empowers our entire psyche. As a result, we naturally play better and take one step toward the state of "on." When we feel alive or in a state of love every dimension of our being is vivified, harmonized, and empowered by that exalted feeling. When we have a deep sense of well-being, everything falls into place. Contrary to this, negative emotions misalign our body and mind and create a lot of discord in our system. In this state there is no flow, there is no game; everything is a struggle and a strain.

> Some higher, harmonizing force is responsible when all our parts are brought together. Sometimes this harmonizing force may be produced by circumstances, as when a strong emotion temporarily integrates us. But if we can increase our ability to

intentionally integrate all our parts into a unified whole we will be masters of ourselves rather than slaves of ego.
(Helminski, *Living Presence*, p. 89)

Self-Consciousness

Susan Jackson lists "loss of self-consciousness" as a quality integral to flow. Maslow describes the qualities of peak experience as being "free of blocks, inhibitions, cautions, fears, doubts, controls, and reservations." Could you talk about how this lack of self-consciousness relates to the state of "on"?

A child who is engrossed in some task lacks this stifling and "boxed-in" sense of self-consciousness. So too does an adult who enters the spirit of an action, who is "all in." Such a person is so fully involved with what he's doing that there's no consciousness left over for him to then *think about* how he might appear to others. This is a state of singularity; it's not disempowered by division, doubt, or an exteriorized consciousness.

All said, when we *think about* ourselves (and how we appear to others) we cannot truly *be* ourselves; we end up living in a mentalized version of life and not in the flow of life itself.

How do we lose this child-like lack of self-consciousness?

We lose it when we lose our direct connection to life; when the aliveness and joy of our own being is supplanted by a mental version of life—one that's founded upon an imagined sense of how we think we appear to others.

As toddlers we are in direct contact with life; we are not thinking about how we appear to others. As children, we begin to see ourselves from the perspective of our parents and shape our actions in accordance with their wants and expectations of us. As teens we start to see ourselves through the eyes of our peers and from some cultural norm. As adults we are firmly locked into seeing and defining ourselves *in accordance with the way we imagine others see us.* Our consciousness is wholly exteriorized (even when we're alone); and we end up living and experiencing life through this mental projection. We think about life, we live through our concept of life, while being in exile from our inherent connection to life and the true aliveness and joy of life. If you want to get biblical about it, we can see this in the story of Adam and Eve. After eating from the tree of knowledge they gain a sense of self and are able to imagine how they might appear from the perspective of another (who happened to be God). It was this ability to create a mental image of self and then to see themselves through the eyes of an imagined other that led them to realize they were naked. But it's not the ability to see ourselves through the eyes of an imagined other that binds us, or the exteriorized image of self we create, but our wholesale identification with that imagined image of self. We are bound when we become who we think we are to others and lose touch with who we really are, who we are to ourselves, to life itself.

We can imaginatively see ourselves through the eyes of others only because we have the cognitive capacity to construct and project a mental representation of ourselves. Small children and animals do not have this cognitive ability. That's why animals are always "on." They're never outside themselves, living through a mental version of self. Have you ever seen a cat hunt? They're never displaced by imagining how others might see them. But human beings always are.

Open and Relaxed Focus

Does the cultivation of a relaxed and open focus (and more attunement to our peripheral vision) help move us into the zone?

It can certainly help. If you focus too intensely on one thing you increase the domination of your cognitive mind (whose stronghold is in the front of the head, around the region of the eyes) and this can block your access to higher modes of awareness. The mode we are looking for is one of diffused, open awareness. This open, non-focused mode decentralizes the cognitive mind and opens you to a higher dimension of self. This same thing can happen when we attune to our peripheral vision; the cognitive mind is diffused and not in total control and this allows more space for our higher mind to enter. [→]

You may notice that most of what you experience in life gets overlaid with some kind of mental commentary. Most people don't actually see (or feel) much; rather they *hear* (and respond to) their conditioned commentary on things. They end up living in their mind and their commentary on what they see (and feel) rather than in the vibrant livingness of life itself. [→]

Can some kind of meditation help with this relaxed focus?

Relaxed focus is another way to describe the employment of your intuitive mind; and, yes, meditation may help shift the nexus of your awareness away from the cognitive mind to your intuitive mind. Only your intuitive mind or higher mind—or what can be understood as you heart mind—is subtle and all-inclusive enough to apperceive your own being.

Rather than using meditation methods, at least in the beginning, I would recommend using the three-fold awareness practice we discussed earlier. This practice involves becoming aware of your breath, your body, and your environment at the same time. Holding three things in your awareness at the same time is something that the cognitive mind cannot do. Try and try as it may, it just can't do it. So, in order to hold these three foci at the same time you must begin to rely upon your intuitive mind. With practice you'll be able to access this mind more and more consistently, and then this heightened state of awareness will begin to emerge during your life and during your game. The state of "on" will feel more and more accessible to you.

Integral Dreamwork

> In a dream, in a vision of the night, when deep sleep falls on men, while they slumber in their beds, He opens their ears and seals their instruction. (Job 33:15-16)

Earlier you mentioned that dreamwork was a powerful way to harmonize the different dimensions of our psyche and move an athlete toward the state of "on." Could you tell us a little more about dreamwork and how it works?

The kind of dreamwork I am most familiar with is an esoteric approach that is different from the more common methods of dream interpretation. This approach is not based on deciphering the symbols in the dream but on unlocking and actuating the dream's higher message or directive.

In general we're very limited in the way we think and act. Our fear-based ego likes to keep things confined, safe, the same, and under its control. That's its primary function. (This ego-function was needed in our early childhood to help insure our survival; but, later, this function becomes the very thing that confines us and keeps us bound to a fearful and immature version of ourselves.) The dream offers you a way to get beyond your ego and its limited way of thinking. It shows you a problem that you try to solve in your normal way—and you fail. Then it shows you the same kind of problem, but stepped up a notch, and you try and fail again. You see, the problem you're presented with in the dream can only be resolved by a higher, more expanded way of thinking and acting. The dream is trying to move you toward this new approach, one that can break you free of your ego and the limits it imposes on you. This is where the dream-master comes in (and you need a dream-master for this kind of work): he knows what your higher self is trying to tell you. He knows the direction it is trying to move you in—and it's always trying to move you toward your higher self. However, your ego sets down a gauntlet of resistance. It throws everything at you—fear, doubt, boredom, discomfort. It's the same stuff the ego has used to control you since you were a child. If, during a dreamwork session, you're finally able to get past your ego defenses, and are able to embrace a higher mode of thinking (and acting), something magical happens—you're suddenly free from all your conceptual constraints and open to the light of your higher self. A profound inner shift and harmonization takes place. Your whole being becomes infused with energy, aliveness, and joy. You're truly able to feel your own wonder and joy. In other words, you're "on."

Team On

> It was basketball but it was friendship more than anything else.
> ~From the movie, *More than a Game*

You spoke about the state of "on" for individuals but what about for a team? Is it possible to move a whole team toward the state of "on"?

When each member of a team has a stronger sense of "we" than of "I" the team naturally moves toward the state of "on." This comes about when there's a true sense of rapport amongst all the members of a team; when it feels more like a family than a team. With this shared sense of "we" everyone is uplifted; everyone feels connected to something greater than himself and everyone plays for something greater than himself.

One way to inspire and build this sense of "we" is for each player to welcome and support everyone on his team *as a person* regardless of their position or level of talent. Rather than coming with judgment or entitlement a player should approach his teammates with mutual respect and heartfelt openness. To be open and truly accepting of others is not always easy. For this a person must get beyond his pettiness and self-concerns; he must stand firm in his own greatness and be able to see and appreciate the greatness in others. This reminds me of another fortune cookie I received, which said, "A truly great man is one who always makes others feel great."

I recently saw the movie Moneyball. *In the system used by Oakland, players were reduced to a number and traded like cattle. Isn't that antithetical to the notion of "we"?*

Yes. And it appears that this number-crunching approach did not work very well. The whole thing turned around after Billy Beane (played by Brad Pitt) talked to his million-dollar player and asked him to interact with the other players (i.e., with the two-hundred thousand dollar players) and become more of a team player. In addition, in order to put his system in place, Beane started interacting with the players; he no longer operated under a negative mindset where he felt he shouldn't interact with players because this would make it more difficult to fire them in the future. Only when Beane went beyond the numbers and his aloof approach and helped create a sense of "we," did the 'A's start winning. The emergence of this sense of "we" was the primary factor in bringing about their success not all that number-crunching.

There's one more thing to note: when the 'A's lost their superstars this was helpful because with that they also lost the very dynamic that was dividing the team and thwarting the emergence of a true sense of "we." The best thing and the worst thing for a team are always its top players. They're best for the team because they're very good players; they're worst for the team because they often come with a sense of entitlement and superiority, and this disrupts the unity of the team.

When a top player feels equal to everyone else, and plays for the benefit of the whole team—and puts more stock in "we" than in "I"—then you have something truly beneficial.

A Simple Lesson Learned

I excelled as a high school soccer player in New Jersey, being named all-state, all-groups, first team in my senior year. However, when I got to Harvard I decided to change my whole relationship to sport: I no longer played to win but for the sheer enjoyment of the game. And so I got into a lot of pick-up soccer games around the Boston area. There was one game I played on a regular basis and, as is always the case, some players had a compatible style with my own and some did not. In particular, I liked playing with a young man from Canada. I regularly found myself as a captain and would always try to get him on my team. He was not the best player on the field, and he was usually selected in the middle of the draw, and when I got my timing right I would pick a few top players and then select him. However, one day my timing was off and my Canadian friend got picked by the other team. On that day I just couldn't connect with the game or my teammates. Everyone seemed to be hogging the ball and playing up front. The game was not much fun either. And of course, we lost. I didn't make that mistake again: I picked my friend much earlier in the draw, even before players that were clearly better than him. And the lesson I learned, which a lot of people already know, is that having a good team, and playing with people you enjoy is often more important (and more often leads to victory) than having the best players on your team. Winning is one thing but winning with your friends and truly enjoying it something else.

Questions & Answers II
The Mental, Physical, and Spiritual Game

I. The Mental Game

Everyone knows the importance of the mental side of sports, so why don't athletes attend to this part of their game with the same diligence as they do their physical game?

This lack of attentiveness may not be due to a lack of desire but more likely to a lack of qualified teachers. There are a lot of knowledgeable athletic coaches who can help you with your physical game but few coaches who know the subtleties of the inner terrain. In addition, to make real gains in the mental game an athlete needs to make fundamental changes in his life and in his relationship to his own mind, and this is often quite difficult. This involves a broader scope of engagement than the physical side of the game. Few athletes are willing or able to put in that kind of effort. They would rather train for hours in the hot sun than do the work required to gain mental mastery.

If someone wants to work on the mental game he may begin by reading a book or two on the subject. However, most of the books out there are in the form of pointers and quick-fix methods—so you're not going to make any major gains with that approach. Mastery of the mental game requires a long, sustained effort; it requires that an athlete make fundamental changes in his value system, his thoughts, and his relationship to life. One-liner techniques and quick-fix approaches will not do; they don't go deep enough. In fact, I was talking with a sports producer the other day who looked over a draft of my book and she told me that most athletes were not going to understand it. She said, "Could you see LeBron James and his teammates reading this book?" So she suggested that I simplify it and "dumb it down"—in other words, make it like all the quick-fix books that are out there. I said that my intention was to try and lift up serious athletes to a higher level of consciousness rather than dumb-down the material for mass appeal. Besides, I think LeBron James could read the book—I mean read it and understand it!

Mental and Physical Coaching

When watching tennis on TV, I sometimes hear the commentator say something like, "this player and his coach don't get along very well" or "they have a stormy relationship." How can such a relationship ever benefit a player and his game?

Well, such a coach might help a player in terms of his physical game but this kind of relationship could never be beneficial to a player's mental game or his long-term relationship to sports and life. Even at the highest level of play there always seems to be a blur between a playing coach and a mental coach; and very often the playing coach becomes the *de facto* mental coach. What this means is that the athlete has no mental coach and no real strategy for working on his mental game—and so his playing coach, who has little or no expertise in this area, steps in to fill the gap.

Some playing coaches try to motivate their players with a kind of "tough love." This may temporarily shift a player toward a more active and focused mode but it will never truly inspire him or move him toward the state of "on." In addition, this "tough love" approach often elicits ill-begotten associations with a critical parent figure and activates deep subconscious defenses—and worse yet, sometimes the mental coach, delivering this tough love, *is* the critical parent!

A coach can also disincline a player from the state of "on" by over-analyzing the player's game or by giving him too many directives to think about. This locks a player into his thinking, cognitive mind and blocks the emergence of his higher, intuitive mind. The primary role of a mental coach is to help a player get control over his mind and emotions; to inspire him; to help him access the source of his own power; to help him build confidence and self-assurance; and to have him be relaxed, focused, and in a state of enjoyment and flow.

Mental Toughness

I often hear people use the phrase "mental toughness" when it comes to the mental game but I've never heard you use that term. Are you teaching something different from that?

I think the cultivation of mental toughness may be a good first step but I don't see it having much to do with the state of "on." I think this term refers to pushing past failures, being able to resist negative emotions, being staunch in the face of adversity, etc. What we're aiming for here is more akin to mental balance, mental flexibility; a state where the cognitive mind is not tough, nor the primary nexus of our action, but where it's translucent, firm but flexible, able to step back and give way to the higher power of your subconscious mind.

The Role of Parents

What is the best role that parents can play, in terms of supporting their children in sports?

The best thing parents can do is support their child with unconditional love, in a way that the child can "get" and appreciate, and never have that love be diminished or dependent on how well their child does in a game or sporting contest. Many young players are distracted and "off their game" when it comes to their parents. Oftentimes they are more concerned about trying to please their parents, or live up to some set of expectations, than with actually playing and enjoying the game. A child's motivation in sport should not be to please his parents (which carries the deep-seated fear that if he does not play well he will be diminished in his parent's eyes and be less loved). And parents often make the mistake of trying to become everything for their child: their coach, their trainer, their friend, their mental coach, etc. This mish-mash of deeply conflicting interests invariable leads to a state of contraction, confusion, and inner dis-integration. That's not what we want.

The only role parents should play is to *unconditionally love and support their child* in his game and in his life. Anything less than that should be counted as a burden.

Mastery and the Subconscious Mind

I would like to know how to open a channel between my conscious intentions and my subconscious mind (as I believe this would help me to master a given action more quickly). Can you talk about how to open this channel or speed up learning?

One thing that speeds up learning and mastery is to truly *enjoy* what you are doing. When your actions are in resonance with your higher nature—i.e., when they are infused with positive qualities such as love, aliveness, euphoria, etc.—they get picked up more quickly by your subconscious mind than actions done half-heartedly, begrudgingly, or without enjoyment.

The channel between our two minds is always open; so the question is, what are you sending (either consciously or unconsciously) through that channel? When you are fully conscious, when you are singular in your intention, when you have entered the spirit of what you are doing, and love what you are doing, that provides a clear and powerful directive to your higher mind. When you practice with this full engagement you're going to master an action a lot faster than when you're just going through the motions of it.

Is there some way we can communicate with our subconscious mind, instructing it to pick up and master certain shots? And would this approach speed up our mastery of the game?

When you accept something you tell your subconscious mind that that is something you want; when you do not accept something you convey the opposite message. So, if you can consciously accept the shots you want (which are all the shots you hit exactly as intended) and consciously not accept the shots you don't want (which are all the shots you miss) you will send a message to your subconscious mind about what you want. When you only accept the shots you want you create *positive shot-templates* for your subconscious mind; and the more you do this the quicker and more powerfully those templates are going to be implemented and the quicker you will master those shots.

You might notice that this is similar to the approach of saying "yes" to positive thoughts (which are the thoughts you want) and "no" to negative thoughts (which are the thoughts you don't want). It's the same thing. We want to accept (or say "yes" to) good shots and not accept (or say "no" to) bad shots. Saying "no" to a bad shot does not mean that you literally say "no," or that you reject the shot, or that you feel bad about it. That's really a "yes" disguised as a "no" because only if you first accept a shot can you then have a negative reaction it. If you don't accept the shot—if you don't identify yourself with hitting the shot—then you would have no reason to feel bad about it, or say "no" to it. *It's not your shot.* It doesn't belong to you. You did not miss it. The shot that went in was your shot.

Sometimes I go to the basketball court and adopt the mindset, "I make every shot"—and then I shoot. I usually make a few shots in a row and feel good about it. Every shot I make confirms this positive sense of self I have (that I am someone who makes every shot). When a shot doesn't go in, I don't react to it because I don't identify with the one who missed the shot. If I am someone who makes every shot, and if a shot did not go in, then *I* could not have taken it. Someone other than "me" missed the shot. Maybe some alien occupied my body in that moment, or maybe some subconscious energy flux took over. I don't know. I don't know who missed that shot but it was not me. I don't even care who missed it; and certainly I would not have any reason to react to the missed shot—because *I did not take it*. I only make shots. I only react to the shots I make. This is the reality I create for myself.

This same approach can also be applied to golf, archery, bowling, volleyball, baseball, etc. In baseball, a player can hold the position of, "I always get a hit." So, when a player comes to bat, or when he's reviewing (and reliving) his times at bat, he would only identify with the player who got a hit. The player who struck out or grounded out or popped out—who was that?

When you're able to adopt this kind of mindset, where you do not lend or apply your sense of "me" to the one who missed the shot (or did not get a hit) you communicate that reality to your subconscious mind. Over time, this is the reality your subconscious mind adopts; and this is the reality that begins to manifest for you. [→]

I don't use this approach all the time; more often I use an attunement approach. This is where I become keenly aware of the shot I missed, comparing everything about it with a perfectly made shot. What was off? Where was my mind at? What was I focusing on? Once I know the characteristics of a missed shot (and also that of a made shot) I'll be in a position to keep inclining myself toward the mental and physical template of a made shot and away from that of a missed shot.

So what we identify with, what we accept, and where we place our sense of "me," is of primary importance?

Yes. And realizing that you have the power to place your attention and your sense of "me" wherever you choose is of equal importance.

As we have said, whatever you identify with, whatever your sense of "me" embraces, whatever feels natural to you, that is what you get. So, you have to identify with and choose that which you want; you have to embrace and embody what you want, now, with every shot. Every time you embrace what you want you tell your subconscious mind, and the universe itself, to give you more of the same in the future. And that's exactly what it sets out to do for you. It will follow your instruction.

Your subconscious mind has one primary function—to support you; and this "you" is determined by *your* sense of "me." Your task, then, is to lend or attach your sense of "me" to that which you want to become. Do you understand? I want to make every shot, I want to hit every ball, so I have to become, and see myself as, someone who makes every shot and hits every ball. Every shot I make is "my shot," and every shot I miss—well, I never miss, so I don't know who took that shot. That's my starting position. That's my communication to my subconscious mind. That's how I play; that's how I live. This is the kind of mindset or mental stance that moves "me" toward what I want rather than trying to move what I want toward my current sense of "me."

II. The Physical Game / Exercise and Fitness

In trying to incline an athlete toward the state of "on" are there some methods of physical training that you recommend and others you advise against?

Yes. In precision sports, such as tennis, golf, baseball, volleyball, basketball (and the positions of quarterback and wide-receiver in football) we don't want to employ gross or what may be called "brutal" exercise methods that tear down or scar the muscle in order to rebuild it stronger. These methods generally dis-coordinate the muscle and throw off the delicate psycho-motor balance of the body. (This has to do with connective tissue and the way it is layered upon a muscle after a hard-core workout; and how that muscle then has to be retrained.) Why did Jelena Jankovic go from being the number one tennis player in the world to all but falling off the wagon the following year? Her answer was that she bulked-up too much during the off-season. And what kind of "bulking up" did she do? Weights. Power-training. All the standard methods. Each time you do power-training and bulk up exercises you have to re-coordinate the whole muscle group and the body in relationship to that muscle group. So the worst thing you can do is power-train for long periods without putting in the practice required to regain your coordination.

Most if not all power-training regimes "dumb-down" the body (including "dumbbells.") The standard use of weights as well as exercise machines and even elastic bands (that increase in resistance the further they are pulled) build muscle at the expense of coordination and balance. A top-ranked player whose game depends upon a high level of precision can be thrown off rather quickly when using these brute-force methods.

The best routine for a precision athlete is one that increases strength and full-body coordination simultaneously. This usually involves a routine where *the entire body is moving and engaged in the exercise* and where the muscles are strengthened and stretched at the same time. Adding "soft" routines to one's workout, such as *chi king* or *hatha yoga*, can help bring about physical and energetic balance (or flow). To increase overall strength and coordination, balance the muscles, and improve the circuitry between both sides of the brain, I have found *The Stick Routine* to be especially useful and somewhat indispensable. This is an isokinetic exercise program I developed about 15 years ago and have been using ever since. [→]

In terms of "on," or moving toward the state of "on," I would have to say that the most important muscle, or muscle group, is the back. When the back is balanced and toned—and working like a well-oiled machine—it rights the vertical axis of the body and brings stability, precision, and power to every movement. So, it is very important to keep the back in perfect shape. In addition to general conditioning, every exercise routine should include "targeted stretching," where each part of the back—upper, middle, and lower—is stretched and toned. (This kind of stretching is most effective when combined with heat and empowered breathing.) Tennis players, who subject themselves to the violent twisting action of the first serve, should keep their back toned and balanced. The same would apply to any sport that involves an imbalance or twisting turn of the back, such as baseball, volleyball, golf, etc. [→]

Optimal Health

We know that fitness is very important in terms of optimal performance but what about good health? Do you have any suggestions for improving overall health?

Fitness is something different from good health although the two are often related. For instance, the better your overall health the fitter you will be in terms of endurance, recovery time, avoidance of injuries, etc. Contrariwise, you can have someone be in really good shape, in terms of muscle tone (and possibly endurance), but be in bad shape in terms of overall health and the condition of their internal organs. (In fact, prolonged endurance training usually depletes the inner organs as vast amounts of energy and bodily resources are shunted outward away from the organs and toward the muscles.)

I know there's a lot of emphasis on vitamins and protein supplements (all of which promise to improve athletic performance) but to get the full benefits from those supplements you must befriend the element of water: you must drink the right kind of water, in the right amount, at the right time. So this is something you want to get right. All forms of chlorine-laced and fluorine-laced tap-water should be avoided. Drinking bottled water (especially when encased in plastic) is not so good either; and it is worse still when exposed to direct sunlight. Apart from artesian well-water, the best water you can drink is water that's been purified through distillation or reverse osmosis and properly revitalized, and stored in a glass or earthenware container. The best way to drink water is in small amounts, at regular intervals—and don't wait until you're thirsty to drink! It's best to drink a half-cup of water every half hour, throughout the day. Water is best when taken at room-temperature or warm. Cold water is not so good. If you're sweating or engaged in rigorous exercise, you'll need to drink more water (and it might be helpful to add in a pinch of Himalayan salt or a few drops of trace minerals to each cup). Adding a small amount of lemon juice to your water is especially good. This helps to alkalinize the body and activate the liver. [→]

Are there any food supplements you recommend?

I'm not into using large amounts of specific vitamins or minerals but I am inclined to use super-foods, food concentrates, or full-spectrum supplements. These might include bee pollen, whey protein concentrate, colloidal minerals, and all those terrible-tasting green drinks (which contain things such as *barley grass juice powder* not ground-up barley grass). Adopting a good, balanced diet, without too much junk food, soda, processed food, wheat and grains, etc. and with the addition of organ meats, especially liver, would be beneficial.

I used to be inclined toward the combination of a sulfur-based protein and flaxseed oil as a way to rejuvenate the body but I'm not so sure about that combination anymore. I also used to put an emphasis on good quality cod liver oil. However, having familiarized myself with the writings of Ray Peat I am now moving away from most if not all PUFAs (polyunsaturated fatty acids) and that includes flaxseed oil, cod liver oil, and the more harmful Omega-6 oils (such as sunflower oil, soybean oil, safflower oil, canola oil, etc.) which are found in chips, fried foods, most baked products, and most processed foods.

Do you have any other health recommendations, in terms of improving oxygenation and circulation?

Several things affect the blood's ability to transport oxygen including pH, hydration, blood-sugar levels, electro-magnetic potential, and blood flow. If your pH levels are too high or too low then the oxygen-carrying ability of your blood is diminished. Likewise, when your blood-sugar levels are too low or too high your blood's ability to transport oxygen is diminished. If your blood doesn't flow well, due to dehydration or a low electro-magnetic charge, it slows oxygen and mineral transport. So make sure you drink small amounts of water throughout the day. You can increase the electro-magnetic charge of your blood by supplementing with lemon juice. [→]

One more thing about oxygen: you can breathe in large amounts of oxygen but if your cells cannot pull in the oxygen then everything comes to naught. Eating the wrong kinds of fats—especially hydrogenated oils, bad PUFAs, preserved meats, and fats that have been corrupted through overheating (such as may be found in fried foods and every manner of corn chip)—ruins the cell's ability to uptake oxygen; whereas eating good fats—including coconut oil, olive oil, and butter—and possibly small amounts of fish oil (from a bottle not a capsule)—can be helpful.

I was watching the Tour de France *the other day and saw a rider drinking Coke during the race. Am I missing something? Isn't Coke about the worse thing an athlete can drink?*

It's about the worse thing *anyone* can drink—but it sure tastes good! One problem with Coke is that it's highly acid-forming. During strenuous exercise (which produces high amounts of acidic waste) high-acidity drinks are the last thing you want to consume because they further decrease the ability of the blood to transport oxygen. The same is true of sugar. High blood-sugar levels cut down on the efficiency of the blood to hold and transport oxygen. And the unnatural spike in blood-sugar levels brought on by soft-drinks wreaks havoc on your pancreas and brings in too much insulin. So, our rider was either ill-advised or the can he was drinking from was filled with pure water (and his team was paid to promote Coke).

All in all, a rider should be drinking pure water (combined with trace minerals and/or lemon juice) and healthy drinks that neutralize acidic waste, provide minerals (in an easy to assimilate form), promote blood-flow (by increasing zeta-potential), and do not cause unnatural blood-sugar spikes.

One thing that decreases oxygen utilization is inflammation. This can come about when strenuous use of the muscles force blood-proteins into the interstitial fluid which then clump together and attract fluid. In order to recover from leg soreness, an athlete should flush out these agglutinated blood-proteins by creating a very slight electrical charge in the muscle and then compressing the muscle (or having it properly massaged). The way to create this charge is to jump up and down for a few seconds or quickly and lightly rubbing your hand over the affected area. This "charging" and lymph drainage could be done between every stage of a race in cycling, between matches in a tennis tournament, or any time when quick recovery is needed.

As a general rule, an athlete should strive to minimized inflammation and avoid foods, substances, and medical interventions that cause inflammation. This may include foods that you are allergic to, including gluten, as well as most PUFAs. It may be good to include foods and supplements that are anti-inflammatory as well, such as CBD oil, turmeric, aspirin, etc.

III. The Spiritual Game

Some athletes pray before a game, either alone or in a group. Is this effective? Is this part of the mental game?

If you believe in the effectiveness of prayer then *by virtue of your belief* it will likely have a positive effect. However, the same could be said about various superstitions and rituals that many athletes have, such as wearing the same pair of trunks for every fight, not shaving for days, eating the same meal before a game, etc. These are effective to the extent that you believe in them. Unfortunately, there is a downside to this: if these rituals are disrupted you may feel it to be a bad omen. And things get really off-kilter when a whole team believes itself to be cursed. For the Boston Red Sox this mass belief became the *Curse of the Bambino*. There was no such curse. The players' subconscious belief in a curse *was* the curse!

But does prayer have power in its own right?

It can, yes. The right kind of prayer can certainly open you up to a higher power and put you in resonance with your higher self. But the bottom line is that *you* have power; *your consciousness* has power in its own right. The power is always yours. Anything that can help you channel and direct *your* consciousness in a positive way has power. As mentioned, there are forms of prayer (or appropriation) that can help you do just that. But true prayer is always a partnership between you and Spirit (or a Higher Power). True prayer is very different from the type of prayer where you beseech a Higher Power to give you something *in the future*. True prayer requires that you appropriate what you want, now. That's the part you are required to play. If you petition a Higher Power for something it's because you feel that something is missing from your life (and that this Higher Power can, if prayed to in the right way, can grant you that missing thing). You're praying because you want something, because you feel the thing you want is missing. Maybe it will be yours in the future, once your prayer is granted, but it's not yours right now. And that belief gets communicated to your higher mind; and then that believed-in "missingness" is what your higher mind sets out to create for you. So be careful with this approach and the mindset upon which it is founded. It may bring you the opposite of what you truly want!

The kind of prayer I've been talking about is not beseeching prayer or petitioning prayer but "creative prayer." This is where you, through the power of your own consciousness, appropriate the state or thing you want, *now*. You don't hope for some future result; you revel in the feeling of having what you want, now. When you feel that you already have what you desire, *now*, the Creative Power moves to manifest your outer conditions so as to correspond with those feelings. It begins with *your* feeling, *your* appropriation of the state you want, now. If you want wealth, abide in the feeling of being wealthy, now; and to do this, the feeling of being wealthy must feel natural to you. If you want victory rejoice in the feeling of victory, now; but to do this, the feeling of victory, and the feeling of being a champion, must feel natural to you. [→]

Bear in mind, we don't get what we want, or wish for, or

think about, or dwell on—or hope will happen in the future—
we get what we are, what feels natural to us, what we believe
ourselves to be. You have to become what you want; you have
to appropriate the state (or feeling) you want. That appropriation, that willingness to experience the state of fulfillment you
want, right now, *is* the prayer. That's the communication to
your higher mind; that's the directive it will follow. And this is
not something new or some New Age concept: this form of
prayer was first mentioned in the New Testament.

> All things whatsoever you pray and ask for, believe that you
> *have* received them [and revel in the feeling of having them
> now] and you *will* receive them. (Mark 11:24)

God's Will

*Some athletes find motivation through their relationship with
God, through doing God's will. Can this be helpful? What does
it mean to do God's will, anyway?*

Anything that you feel positive about, anything that increases your sense of self, your enthusiasm, and your aliveness
can be helpful, and for many people this is found in their relationship with God. This is a very personal issue and there's no
right answer; but what I can do is offer my perspective on this.
According to some spiritual traditions, the primary Will of God
(or Spirit) is to know and experience more and more of His
own nature, more and more of His own qualities, more and
more of what He feels Himself to be. This is the Primary Will
that brings the entire universe into existence. Stated more specifically, we could say that the Will of God (i.e., the will that
God has for Himself) is to experience more and more of His
own aliveness, love, abundance, peace, beauty, etc., through
the various forms of creation. Now if this is the will that God
has for Himself it must be the will He has for all of us as well.

Accordingly, our will (and desire) to know our highest good, to experience more and more of our inherent joy, aliveness, beauty, etc., is God's Will for us. It is God's Will experienced through our individual nature.

The fundamental error that most human beings make is not that they ask for too much but for too little. Spirit (or God) always wants the highest and greatest for you. Truly wanting the same for yourself and always orienting yourself in that direction is what it means to do the highest will.

So, according to this view, it's God's will that we know more and more of our own love, joy, and aliveness?

Yes. The highest will is that we know and express all the pristine qualities of our nature; that we ever unfold into the beauty and livingness of Life. This, we could say, is our birthright. But we have to get beyond the limiting constraints of our mind and get in touch with our own nature before we can truly do that. Living in and through a flat, mentalized version of life, where we are never truly in touch with our own nature or Life itself, just won't do. That's "off." We don't want to be off—off our game, off our heart, and off our own life. We want to be "on." Being "on," being in a state where we experience *and enjoy* our highest qualities is what it means to do God's Will. That's the way I see it. That's the way I live it.

All said, then, God (or Spirit) wants us to be "on" all the time?

Yes—in flow with life, in oneness with joy, in the ever-expanding wonder of our own being. That's the way God lives. If we are the children of God, in oneness with God, tell me, how could God want anything different for us?

APPENDIX

Appendix:
Guidelines for Conscious Retrieval

Below are some guidelines for a session of *Conscious Retrieval* (which can also be used for *Creative Revision*).

Each session should take place in a clean, safe, and quiet environment. (For purposes of explanation, the person going through the process is the "Imaginative Recaller" or IR; and the person helping him is the "Assistant.") During a session, the IR should sit upright in a chair (with his eyes closed) across from the Assistant, who is also in a chair. The Assistant's role is to help the IR recall the painful incident as fully as possible while remaining neutral and "invisible," and never judging, commenting upon, or reacting to anything stated by the IR. The Assistant should never use the word "I" or make any reference to himself. Confidentiality is of the utmost importance: The IR must trust the Assistant and feel safe in his company. The Assistant should never talk about the session, or anything that occurred in the session to the IR or anyone else. The IR should be alert and relaxed, and without agitation or fatigue.

A Typical Session
1. Assistant: "We're going to begin this session of Conscious Retrieval. Are you relaxed and ready to begin?" (IR: "Yes.") "OK, locate a painful incident that you want to work through at this time." IR locates an incident.

2. Assistant: "Once you have a clear incident in mind, go to the beginning; re-enter the incident and describe it as it is happening right now." The IR describes the incident, from the beginning to the end, as it is happening in his imagination.

3. Assistant: "OK, go back to the beginning of the incident and describe it again; see if there are any more details you can pick up." The Assistant wants to make sure that the IR is not simply recalling the event from an outside position but actually reliving and re-experiencing it in the now. The Assistant might

say, "Make sure you are in the event; that you are feeling and responding to the event as it is happening right now."

When the Assistant hears the IR's description, and believes he may be skipping over important details, he may direct the IR to pick up more sensations. He would ask: "What sounds do you hear?" "What words are being spoken?" "What physical sensations are you experiencing?" "Is there any particular smell in the air?" (The Assistant may ask questions that help the IR recall sensations he is overlooking but he must not direct the IR in any direction other than where the IR is going.)

4. After the IR finishes recalling the event, the Assistant directs him to re-enter it again: "OK, go back to the beginning of the incident and see if there are any additional details you can recall." After a few times the IR may begin to resist the procedure and not want to re-live the traumatic incident again. This is a typical ego-defense. The Assistant must "stick to his guns" and have the IR re-live the incident, even if he does not want to. This resistance may be the very thing the IR's ego is using to avoid experiencing the pain of the original event. The Assistant may have him re-live the event ten or more times. So long as new information is being picked up by the IR, the Assistant has him go over the incident again.

5. If the IR is not getting any more details, and has not experienced any discharge of pain, you can suspect that the event being recalled is being sustained by an earlier trauma. If this is the case, the Assistant may ask: "Can you recall an earlier incident that is similar to this one?" If the IR recalls an earlier incident, then the Assistant has him go to the beginning of that event and re-enter it as he did the first, going over it again and again until it is fully recalled and relived, and its negative emotional charge is dissolved.

6. After about 40 to 90 minutes, or when the IR comes to some kind of resolution or natural stopping place (which usually happens when the emotional charge of a traumatic event is discharged) the Assistant calls an end to the session.

The IR has been in a state of reverie or "imaginative recall," which is similar to a state of meditation, and he needs to be brought out gently. To mark the end of the session the Assistant may ring a bell or gently say that the session is over. After this, the IR can open his eyes and return to the present moment.

Bibliography

Adyashanti. *The Impact of Awakening*. Los Gatos, California: Open Gate Publishing, 2000.

Bayda, Ezra. *Zen Heart*. Boston: Shambhala, 2008.

Cooper, Andrew. *Playing in the Zone*. Boston: Shambhala, 1998.

Douillard, John. *Body, Mind, and Sport*. New York: Three Rivers Press, 2001.

Goddard, Neville. *The Neville Reader*. Camarillo, California: DeVorss, 2005.
―――――. *The Power of Awareness*. Camarillo, California: DeVorss, 1952.

Hawkins, David. *Power Vs Force*. Carlsbad, California: Hay House, 2002.

Helminski, Kabir. *Living Presence*. New York: Putnam, 1992.

Pelé. *My Life and the Beautiful Game. New York:* Doubleday, 1977.

Russell, Bill. *Second Wind*. New York: Ballantine, 1980.

Troward, Thomas. *The Hidden Power*. NY: McBride & Co., 1922.

About the Author

Jonathan Star is a well-known author and spiritual teacher. For over twenty years he has been involved with the practice of yoga, meditation, and the healing sciences; and has taught meditation and *chi gung* in the USA, Europe, and Asia. He graduated from Harvard College with a degree in psychology. His books include, *The Inner Treasure*, *Rumi: In the Arms of the Beloved*, and *Tao Te Ching: The Definitive Edition*.

GameOnLife.weebly.com
JonathanStar.com